Contents

9 FORWARD

11 WELCOME

20 APPROACHING THE CATHEDRAL
27 The West Façade

30 THE MAIN LEVEL
30 The Narthex
34 The Crossing
37 The Rose Windows
40 The High Altar and the Great Choir
46 The Nave Chapels
53 The Transepts
58 The Nave
63 Presidential Memorials
67 Architectural and Decorative
Carvings in the Nave
68 Other Points of Interest

70 THE LOWER LEVEL
70 The North and South Crypt Aisles
75 The Chapel of the Good Shepherd
75 Bethlehem Chapel
77 The Chapel of St. Joseph of Arimathea
78 The Chapel of the Resurrection
80 The Cathedral Center for
Prayer and Pilgrimage

82 THE EXTERIOR
84 The Central Tower
87 The North Porch and the Garth
88 The Apse
88 The South Portal
90 The West Towers
90 The Cathedral Close
95 The Bishop's Garden and
the Herb Cottage
96 Olmsted Woods and the Pilgrim Steps

98 BUILDING THE CATHEDRAL
A history of Cathedral construction

106 THE LIVING CATHEDRAL
A photographic essay

128 GENERAL INFORMATION
129 Chronology of Notable Events
132 Glossary of Terms
134 Bishops of the Episcopal
Diocese of Washington
134 Deans of Washington
National Cathedral
135 Interred at the Cathedral
136 For Further Reading
137 Great Cathedrals
138 Diagram of Exterior
140 Cross Section of Nave
140 Construction Timeline
141 Nave Elevations
142 Main Level Floor Plan
143 Lower Level Floor Plan
144 Map of the Close

SIDEBARS
32 *Symbolism in the Shield*
38 *Transcendence Through Color and Light*
43 *Giving Praise Through Music*
44 *Intricacies in Iron*
49 *The Nation's Church*
53 *Beauty in the Details*
56 *A Cathedral for All People*
65 *Anomalies of Architecture*
72 *Living Stones*
77 *A Stitch in Time*
79 *Casting Light and Good*
91 *Curious Creatures*
92 *Carvers of Stone*
94 *Continuing the Legacy*

Forward

Welcome to Washington National Cathedral, a house of worship for all people and the seat of the Episcopal Bishop of Washington and the Presiding Bishop and Primate of the Episcopal Church. We are also known as the Church of Saint Peter and Saint Paul, named after two influential leaders of the early church. Peter was given the charge by Christ to be the first leader of the early Christian community, and Paul the Apostle, a convert to the faith, was the first theologian of the Christian Church. The two great towers at the Cathedral's west façade are named for these two faithful leaders and are a testament to their influence on the formation of the early church.

In 2007, we marked the 100th anniversary of the laying of the cornerstone of this, the sixth largest cathedral in the world. With the second century upon us, the Cathedral now more than ever holds a special place in the life of the city of Washington, the nation, and the world. The Cathedral is a center for worship, ministry, spiritual growth, education, interfaith dialogue, and stimulating ecumenical discourse. It is a partner with other great cathedrals throughout the world in seeking reconciliation and peace in a too often violent and broken world. Each day the message of God's unconditional love for the whole of creation is prayed for, preached, taught, and lived out within the life of Washington National Cathedral. We invite you to join us in this mission; a mission that is truly centered here in this holy place.

Every year over three-quarters of a million people visit the Cathedral as worshippers and pilgrims to experience the art, architecture, educational programs, music, and worship life that are unique to Washington National Cathedral. We invite you to join us in the Cathedral's great offerings and to experience firsthand the profound beauty and holiness of this sacred space.

—The Right Reverend John Bryson Chane, D.D.
Eighth Bishop of Washington
Chief Executive Officer of the Protestant Episcopal Cathedral Foundation

Welcome

WELCOME TO WASHINGTON NATIONAL CATHEDRAL. Through this guide you are entering not only a national architectural treasure, but a holy place with a special historic mission. Begun in 1907, the Cathedral was chartered by Congress, and was envisioned by its founders to be a spiritual home for the nation embracing all faiths. In addition to being a beautiful structure, the National Cathedral is the place where some of the great voices of our time have offered inspiring and challenging words calling America, and each of us individually, to lives of generosity and compassion, and to fulfill God's dream of a hopeful and peaceful world for everyone. In addition to presidents and prominent clergy of all faiths, such distinguished world leaders as Dr. Martin Luther King, Jr., the Dalai Lama, and Archbishop Desmond Tutu have used our Canterbury Pulpit as a platform to call the nation and the world to the work of justice and reconciliation.

Cathedrals are full of stories told through art and architecture, as well as through music and worship. In every arch and chapel, every statue and window, we can see the story of God's presence in human history as experienced in the Hebrew and Christian traditions—through sacred events, holy prophets and leaders, and through the ongoing struggle of people of faith to love and serve the God of the universe. And because this is a national cathedral, these walls contain much of the American story as well. This guidebook is designed to help you understand our glorious stained glass windows, artwork, and worship spaces, and even to illuminate those peculiar gargoyles perched on our outside walls, gazing over the city of Washington.

Please visit us often, on-line and in person, and join the hundreds of thousands of people each year who have been touched by this holy space. A century of faith, craft, and determined labor raised the Cathedral; but long before the last stone was put in place, our forebears directed the Cathedral's mission outward to serving the city, the nation, and the world. Our second century will continue the work of the first, as we seek to be a catalyst for hope, healing, and reconciliation. Please stay in touch, no matter where you live, and please consider joining us in support of this vital ministry of serving as a spiritual home for the nation.

May God bless you through your encounter with Washington National Cathedral.

—THE VERY REVEREND SAMUEL T. LLOYD III
Dean, Washington National Cathedral

It's wonderful to climb
the liquid mountains o
Behin
and I have no fears.

*BEYOND THE BUSTLE
OF KEY BRIDGE AND
GEORGETOWN, WASHINGTON
NATIONAL CATHEDRAL
GRACES THE CITY'S SKYLINE.*

the sky
me and before me is God

Religion points to that area of
human experience
where in one way or another
man comes upon mystery
as a summons to pilgrimage.

— FREDERICK BUECHNER

✣ LEFT: *ACROSS THE CITY, TO THE SOUTH OF THE CATHEDRAL STANDS THE NEOCLASSICAL MEMORIAL BRIDGE, A SYMBOL OF THE NATION'S RECONCILIATION FOLLOWING THE CIVIL WAR.*

✣ ABOVE: *SNOWY BRANCHES GIVE WAY TO THE CATHEDRAL'S TOWERS, GOLDEN IN THE AFTERNOON SUN.*

✦ RISING ABOVE THE CITY'S
CHANGING LANDSCAPE, THE
OLD POST OFFICE FACES
WASHINGTON CATHEDRAL,
TWO CONSTANTS IN THE
CITY'S NEW CENTURY.

foundations of a person
are not in matter
but in spirit.

—RALPH WALDO EMERSON

Impart as much as you can of
your spiritual being to those
        who are on the road with you,
and accept as something precious
   what comes back to you from them.

— ALBERT SCHWEITZER

✣ ABOVE: *IN MAY 2008,*
THE CATHEDRAL BECAME
A BEACON OF HOPE AND
RECONCILIATION, AS SWISS
LIGHTING ARTIST GERRY
HOFSTETTER TRANSFORMED
THE CATHEDRAL'S FAÇADE
WITH HIS GLORIOUS
REPRESENTATIONS.

✣ RIGHT: *THE COMMU-*
NITY OF NORTHWEST
WASHINGTON, WITH ITS
HOMES AND SHOPS,
ENFOLDS THE CATHEDRAL
IN ITS DAY-TO-DAY LIFE.

✤ *From the verdant dark green of Olmsted Woods, the Cathedral appears a contrasting landscape of shadows and light.*

Approaching the Cathedral

FROM A DISTANCE, Washington National Cathedral extends above the tree line of Washington's Mount St. Alban with a majestic elegance, attracting the gaze of the lifelong resident and the first-time visitor alike, inspiring a quiet awe. To all, the image beckons in a timeless visual language. The Cathedral, with its expanse of stone and three soaring towers, is visible for many miles in any direction, invoking the glory and mystery of God that invites all people to approach.

To draw nearer to the Cathedral is to relinquish the dictates of daily life. Here, the tedium of the workaday world is overcome by the

assertions of faith and the majestic structure: From the enormous height of the
columns that draw the eye upwards toward
heaven to the jewel-like windows casting
light on the stones below, every element of
construction is designed to reveal the presence of God and to teach humankind the
mysteries of faith. God is glorified in every
block of limestone and shard of glass, every
gray shadow and glint of light, every arch
and spire, every niche and portal.

Its very name, Washington National
Cathedral, bespeaks its role as a national
church, one where people of all religions
and those exploring spirituality can come
together to celebrate the events that shape a nation. A site
for a church "for national purposes" was incorporated into
the 1791 plans for the Federal City prepared by Pierre L'En-
fant. A century later, the Cathedral's founders determined to
build an Episcopal cathedral that would serve as a gathering
place for the nation in times of mourning and of celebration.
In 1893 President Benjamin Harrison signed the Congres-
sional charter that incorporated the Protestant Episcopal
Cathedral Foundation "to establish within the District of
Columbia a cathedral and institutions of learning for the

✤ ABOVE: *THE SUN
RISES OVER THE CITY OF
WASHINGTON, THROWING
A SOFT PINK LIGHT ON
THE CATHEDRAL'S LIME-
STONE TOWERS.*

✤ RIGHT: *WHEN THE
CATHEDRAL'S FOUND-
ATION STONE WAS LAID
IN 1907, WISCONSIN
AVENUE WAS ONLY A DIRT
ROAD. TODAY, IT'S A MAIN
THOROUGHFARE, BRING-
ING VISITORS FROM ALL
OVER THE WORLD TO THE
CATHEDRAL.*

✢ ABOVE: *ST. PETER, WHOM JESUS CALLED TO BE A "FISHER OF MEN," GAZES TOWARDS ETERNITY FROM THE WEST FAÇADE OF THE CATHEDRAL.*

✢ RIGHT: *A CLEAR NIGHT SKY FRAMES THE ELEGANT SYMMETRY OF THE CATHEDRAL'S FLYING BUTTRESSES AND THE ORNATE MAJESTY OF ITS TOWERS.*

promotion of religion and education and charity." Two years later, the Episcopal Diocese of Washington was created.

Planning for construction of the Cathedral began immediately, but it would take almost a century to build it. The efforts of people from all walks of life contributed to the completion of the structure: the vision of bishops, deans, and architects; the talents of artists and craftspeople; the management of clergy and lay leaders; and the financial support of private citizens throughout the nation.

The Gothic cathedral that took shape above the city has been remarkable for its ministry, as well as its architecture. The first Episcopal Bishop of Washington, Henry Yates Satterlee (1843–1908), was a dedicated ecumenist who believed in cooperation among religions. It was his determination that the Cathedral should be a "House of Prayer for all People."

Those words, emblazoned on the Cathedral banner, express this church's welcome to people of all faiths and those of no particular affiliation.

A Gothic cathedral is meant to instruct as well as inspire. The iconography of a cathedral is the system of images and symbols used in sculptures, stained glass, and other art forms to tell the Christian story. The Cathedral's iconography is depicted in works of art that fall into three categories: the symbolic presentation of the invisible God; the presentation of a biblical theme or belief; and the representation of the history of the Christian church and those who express their faith through good works.

As with the medieval Gothic cathedrals, the iconography of Washington National Cathedral interprets the word of God in the human world. In keeping with ancient church

feet above sea level, making its top the highest point in the District of Columbia. In 2007, the American Institute of Architects released a list of "America's Favorite Architecture," on which list the Cathedral ranked third, after the Empire State Building and the White House. The Cathedral welcomes some 750,000 visitors and worshippers annually, and hundreds of thousands more worldwide on its website.

THE WEST FAÇADE

While there are numerous ways to enter this sacred structure, only at the majestic west façade does the Cathedral proclaim itself most fully to approaching visitors. To stand before the west façade is to face east, towards the rising sun, the new day, towards Jerusalem, and, in the more immediate terms of the building's structure, towards the High Altar and its declaration of the risen Christ. The Cathedral's dramatic vertical proportion, accentuated by twin towers and anchored by single-story wings at its base, its large rose window and three portals sheltered by pointed arches, and the stately simplicity of its decorative scheme are a statement of profound respect for the religious tradition the Cathedral seeks to sustain. Unmistakably Gothic in architectural style, the façade establishes an expectation of the austere beauty and serene order to be experienced within in the continued iconographic portrayal of the biblical story.

As with its great medieval forebears, the Cathedral's west front marks a boundary: its portals present a metaphorical gateway into the Christian story. But the Cathedral proclaims its position as a new church in a New World by breaking with the tradition of marking that boundary with forbidding images of the Last Judgment or of the earthly deaths of Jesus Christ and the saints of the Church. Instead of the solemn warnings favored in earlier centuries, the sculpture of the Cathedral's west portals suggests a theology of spiritual rebirth and portrayal of the creation of the world and of humanity, as told in the Book of Genesis. To enter the Cathedral, then, is to embark on a journey, a new beginning. In contrast to the often extravagantly carved façades of the European cathedrals of earlier centuries, Washington National Cathedral is striking in

✤ *A WONDROUS COMPO-SITION OF ANGLES, ARCHES, RECTANGLES, AND CIRCLES, THE DESIGN FOR THE WEST FAÇADE WAS CHANGED REPEATEDLY BY ARCHITECT PHILIP FROHMAN, IN HIS QUEST FOR PERFECTION.*

north tympanum represents the *Creation of Day*, the creation of the seen aspects of the universe. The creation of the unseen aspects of the universe is represented in the south portal tympanum, entitled *Creation of Night*.

The towers that dominate the west façade are dedicated to the two saints for whom the Cathedral is formally named. Accordingly, Hart's trumeau sculptures for the side portals are statues of these founders of the Christian tradition, the apostles Peter and Paul. In the north portal, beneath *Creation of Day*, is the sculpture of St. Peter. Eyes lifted to the horizon and the empty fishing net over his shoulder suggest the beginning of his sojourn as a "fisher of men." Beneath the *Creation of Night* in the south portal stands the figure of St. Paul. Depicted at the moment of his conversion to Christianity, when temporarily struck blind by the power of God, his pose echoes those of the figures in *Ex Nihilo*.

The dedication of *Ex Nihilo* in May of 1982 coincided with the seventy-fifth anniversary celebration of the Cathedral. The occasion marked the completion of the west façade sculptures, almost a decade of work by Hart, master carvers Vincent Palumbo (1936–2000) and Roger Morigi (1907–1995), and their assistants. Palumbo, joined by Walter Arnold, Gerald Lynch, and Patrick Plunkett, had spent two years carving, *in situ*, the *Ex Nihilo* tympanum, perched atop scaffolding, translating into stone some twenty plaster models into which the monumental panel had been subdivided. But it was carving the figure of St. Peter that Palumbo, whose career at the Cathedral spanned almost four decades, considered his masterwork. The carving of the figure of Adam was the final project for Morigi, bringing to a close in 1978 more than two decades of his work at the Cathedral.

Monumental pierced bronze gates by German sculptor Ulrich Henn (b. 1925) complete each portal and support the themes of the sculpture of the west façade. Their lacelike and organic forms, inspired by plants native to the New World, establish a sense of welcoming openness, a striking contrast to the heavy and forbidding doors typical of great cathedrals of the past. In the gates of the central portal are roundels recounting stories of the patriarchs, Abraham and Moses, and portions of the Genesis and Exodus narratives. The north pair tells the story of Abraham and Isaac, while the south pair presents important moments in the life of Moses. The gates of the north and south portals depict events in the lives of St. Peter and St. Paul, respectively. ▪

the restraint of its ornamentation. Niches, which might be filled with portraits of heroes or martyrs of the past, remain empty.

Figuratively carved detail is limited to a group of works known as the *Creation Sculptures,* by sculptor Frederick Hart (1943–1999). Hart began his extraordinary career at the Cathedral as an apprentice stone carver, doing office work while observing and learning his craft. From these humble beginnings and through persistence, he was awarded what has come to be regarded as one of the most important commissions of religious sculpture of the twentieth century. Crowning each of the three portals is a deeply carved tympanum sculpture representing an aspect, not of death, but of Creation. In the center, a work entitled *Ex Nihilo* captures the dawning of humankind, in which half-formed figures of men and women emerge from the void. Beneath this expressive carving stands the figure of Adam, the first man, his eyes not yet open and his body not yet fully freed from the surrounding stone. Hart's sculpture for the

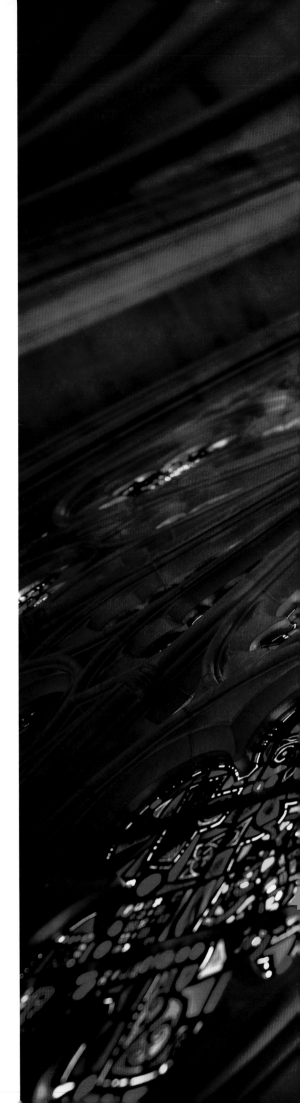

The Main Level

TO ENTER THE CATHEDRAL is to be invited to experience a world beyond everyday concerns, to step through its portals into the realm of the eternal, and to discover, in the layered richness of its sacred imagery, the story and meaning of the Christian faith. From west to east, from the bronze of the entry gates to the stones of the High Altar, from the Creation of humankind to the reign in majesty of its Redeemer, the Cathedral interior and its every facet are called into service of the Cathedral's mission to boldly proclaim its message of faith, to affirm its teachings, to intrigue the novice, to inspire the faithful, and to glorify God.

THE NARTHEX

Beyond the bronze gates of the west portals, the transition from the secular world to the spiritual world is mediated by the narthex, or entryway, by which one approaches the Cathedral nave. With its reduced light and scaled-down dimensions, the narthex urges the visitor to set aside the worries of the workaday world and to prepare, both physically and spiritually, for entry into a consecrated space. Above the doors leading to the nave, unusual leaded windows

✤ *The core of sculptor Theodore Barbarossa's illustrations of the Decalogue, above the west balcony, is the massive boss depicting Moses, the Lawgiver.*

designed by Robert Pinart (b. 1927) contribute to the experience of transition. Made of hand-blown clear glass, the abstract windows distort the view into the nave, reflecting the mystery of faith and thereby enhancing the experience of moving into a place set apart for and dedicated to God.

Other details of the narthex announce the Cathedral's identity as a spiritual home for the nation: The floor in the narthex is decorated with a mosaic of state seals. The seals of every state and the District of Columbia surround the Great Seal of the United States. Just beyond the center doors, the shield of the Cathedral, with the crossed keys of St. Peter and the sword of St. Paul, is set into the floor. This marble seal was laid in the presence of Queen Elizabeth II and President Gerald Ford at the time of the dedication of the nave in 1976.

In contrast to the tempering confines of the narthex, the majestic space of the nave opens both vertically and horizontally, revealing a spiritually powerful interplay of line and color, shadow and light. Just as the majestic towers of the exterior lift the gaze of the earthbound toward heaven, the soaring piers of the interior raise tons of stone in a gracefully articulated canopy of arching vaults over dazzling vistas of stained glass and then eastward into the nave's deep expanse. Through the nave, past the crossing, beyond the choir and into the sanctuary, the central message of both the building and the faith it represents is revealed in the gleaming image of the *Majestus* above the High Altar: the enthroned figure of Jesus the Christ.

The very word "nave," which refers to the main body of a church, excluding the transepts (the side arms) and the apse (containing the choir and High Altar), derives from the Latin word for ship. The church building is the symbolic ship in which the followers of Christ travel toward salvation. It is, therefore, in the nave where the unity of the Cathedral's iconography is most apparent. The images in stained glass, carved stone, and wrought iron convey the story of God's covenant with the Hebrew people, the promise of redemption through God made flesh, and its fulfillment in the person of Jesus Christ.

The Clerestory Windows

The Cathedral's foremost stained glass artist, Rowan LeCompte (b. 1925), once likened stained glass to music: "Both are emotional and instantly perceived," he said. "Like music, stained glass can stimulate the imagination, it can lift the heart, it can enchant." The dynamic bursts of color that suffuse the nave's space immediately engage the visitor on a visceral level. The tallest and largest of the nave windows are the four-lancet clerestory windows, eighteen in all, and each designed by LeCompte. As they imbue the nave with light and color, they also unfold their portion of the Cathedral's iconographic scheme, portraying the progress of the Hebrew people as God prepared them for the coming of

SYMBOLISM IN THE SHIELD

The coat of arms of the Church of St. Peter and St. Paul of the Episcopal Diocese of Washington was designed in 1949 by Alanson H. Sturgis of Sturgis Associates, Inc., Boston. The field of shield is red, symbolizing courage and loyalty. In the center of the shield are the crossed keys of St. Peter and the sword of St. Paul. The hilted sword is placed with the point up, signifying victory. The handle of each key is made of two fish, an ancient Christian symbol signifying Christ. The keys and sword pass through a golden crown, which has three meanings: the martyrdom of the two saints, the sovereignty of Christ, and the location of the Cathedral in our nation's capital, where the sovereign government is established. Above the shield are the mitre, key, and pastoral staff, which symbolize the authority and jurisdiction of the bishop.

the Messiah. Starting at the west end, the first pair represents God's gift to humanity of the earth for shelter and sustenance. Moving east, the second pair signifies God's covenant with the Hebrew people. The third pair represents the passage of time and the history of the Hebrews. The suffering and redemption in the life of the Hebrews is the theme of the fourth pair. In the fifth pair, reform and growth in the Hebrew nation are highlighted. The sixth pair symbolizes the Hebrew faith. The theme of the seventh pair is religion and righteousness, as set down in the first and second commandments, and in the eighth pair the coming of the Messiah is foretold. With the ninth pair, which portrays the conversions of Peter (north) and Paul (south), the transition from the Hebrew Bible to the New Testament is complete.

The Boss Stones

Progressing from a statement of Creation at the Cathedral's west front, the iconography of the nave is a carefully orchestrated celebration of history, a proclamation of the birth of a new faith, and a demonstration of the flowering of that faith in the works of men and women through the ages. It is instructive that a group of stones that are among the most

important to the structural integrity of the nave, some weighing as much as five tons, is carved with imagery representing laws and beliefs that are the most important to the spiritual integrity of the Christian faith. Called boss stones, these are visible high overhead, where the ribs of the vaulted ceilings converge. Without these key load-bearing stones, the massive weight of the ceiling could not be suspended for such immense spans. One of the rare and special features of the architecture of Washington National Cathedral is that its many boss stones, some 762 in all, are each uniquely carved with symbolic and decorative imagery. Only the fourteenth-century cathedral of Norwich, in England, has more such boss carvings.

The Cathedral's largest boss stone, which is nearly five feet in diameter, occupies a position of importance in the vaulting over the west balcony, directly above the central portal into the nave. It is carved with the image of Moses, the lawgiver, holding the tablets inscribed with the Ten Commandments given by God to the people of Israel. The

❖ *THE SOARING ARTISTRY OF THE NAVE'S STAINED GLASS, GOTHIC VAULTING, AND BOSS CARVINGS STANDS WITNESS TO THE HUMAN ASPIRATION TO PRAISE GOD THROUGH CREATIVE EXPRESSION.*

carvings in ten bosses surrounding this stone represent each of the commandments.

Proceeding from these stones are the creedal boss stones, which span the ridgeline of the Cathedral parallel to the center aisle. Just as the statements of the Nicene and Apostles' creeds provide the theological framework upon which the Christian Church is built, so too do these boss stones delineate the structural backbone of the Cathedral. It is, therefore, fitting that the affirmations of the creeds inspire the imagery of the twenty-four main bosses. They begin at the west end with, "I believe in God the Father almighty," (the opening words of the Apostles' Creed). They conclude above the High Altar with the final affirmation of the Nicene Creed, "I believe in the life of the world to come," inscribed in another of the largest of the carved Cathedral boss-es. Interspersed between these boss stones, subordinate bosses expand upon ideas found in the two creeds.

THE CROSSING

Cathedrals are great houses of worship and centers for inspiring liturgies and public services. More than 1,500 services are held in the Cathedral each year. Many of these take place in the crossing, which, in any cruciform church or cathedral, is the square space formed by the intersection of the nave, the chancel, and the transepts. Both structurally and theologically, the crossing is the center of the Cathedral's worship and community life.

At each of the four corners of the crossing stand four mammoth piers soaring high into the shadows ninety-eight feet overhead. From their bases deep beneath the Cathedral, the piers are 324 feet high. At the crossing the piers are nineteen feet in diameter; in the crypt, in the Chapel of St. Joseph of Arimathea directly below, they are twen-ty-seven feet in diameter. Their solid masonry construction supports the Gloria in Excelsis tower and its two sets of bells, a fifty-three-bell carillon and a ten-bell peal used in the traditional art of change ringing.

THIS ALTAR PLAT-FORM AT THE CROSSING REFLECTS THE MISSION OF DEAN SAMUEL T. LLOYD III "TO ENGAGE THE CONGREGATION MORE FULLY IN THE WORSHIP EXPERIENCE."

The Pulpit and the Lectern

The focal point of the crossing is the Canterbury Pulpit, from which the sermon is preached during services. Placed to the right of the High Altar, as you face the choir, this ornately carved pulpit asserts the Cathedral's commitment to the spoken word. United States presidents and prominent faith leaders have spoken from here, among them former president Jimmy Carter, the Rev. Billy Graham, Archbishop Desmond Tutu, and the Dalai Lama. From this place, on March 31, 1968, the Rev. Dr. Martin Luther King, Jr., delivered his last Sunday sermon before he was assassinated four days later.

You cut and cut and all of a sudden you see something grow. The more you work, the better it comes out. You feel good inside. You work, it gets brilliant, you see it move. It fills you with some kind of emotion— such a sense of satisfaction.

—ROGER MORIGI
Master Carver

This pulpit was one of the first furnishings given to the Cathedral. Before construction of the Cathedral had begun, Henry Yates Satterlee, the first Bishop of Washington, set about acquiring stones from sacred sites in the Holy Land and England that could be fashioned into such essential liturgical furnishings as the High Altar, baptismal font, cathedra, and pulpit. With that goal in mind, Satterlee accepted a gift from the Archbishop of Canterbury of stones from the sixteenth-century Bell Harry Tower of Canterbury Cathedral, which had undergone repair and restoration in the 1880s. Designed by the English architect W. Douglas Caroe from a sketch created by Bishop Satterlee and carved in England, the Canterbury Pulpit, which stands ten feet high, depicts the history of the English translations of the Bible. Each of its three carved panels portrays an illustrious church leader: the Venerable Bede (673–735), a Benedictine monk and church historian, dictating

on his death bed a translation of the Gospel according to St. John into Anglo-Saxon; Stephen Langton (1150–1228), Archbishop of Canterbury, with the barons at Runnymede, handing the Magna Carta to King John for his signature; and the martyrdom of William Tyndale (ca. 1494–1536), who was burned at the stake for his pioneering efforts to translate, print, and distribute the entire Bible in English.

The four statues separating the panels represent other men who are identified with the translation of the Bible into English: King Alfred the Great (871–899), who gave his people the Ten Commandments and the Lord's Prayer in their own language; John Wycliffe (1330–1384), whose Bible was issued in 1383; Lancelot

✤ *IN THE LAST SUNDAY SERMON HE PREACHED, MARTIN LUTHER KING, JR., LOOKED OUT OVER A PACKED CATHEDRAL AND EXPRESSED HIS DELIGHT AT "STANDING IN THIS VERY GREAT AND SIGNIFICANT PULPIT."*

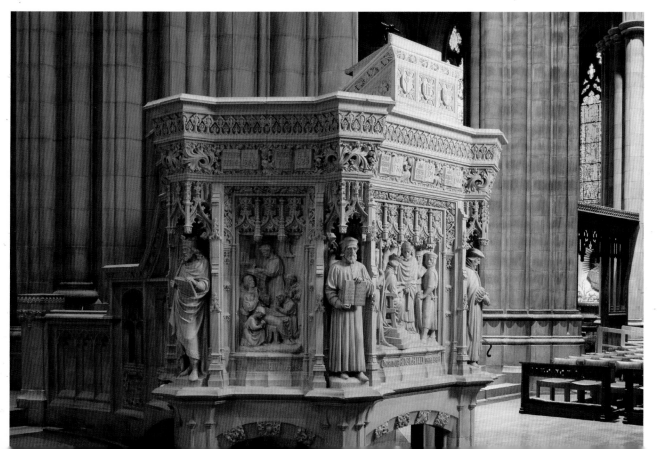

Andrewes (1555–1626), Bishop of Winchester, foremost trans- lator of the 1611 King James Version; and Brooke Foss Westcott (1825–1901), Bishop of Durham, who was a leader in the com- pany that set forth the revised version in 1881.

To the left is the lectern, from which the Holy Bible is read during services. The canopied niches on the lectern depict seven men who recorded the Word of God: Moses (the law), David (the Psalms), Elijah (the Prophets), St. Luke (the Gospels), Sts. Peter and Paul (the Epistles), and St. John (the Book of Revelation).

The Rood Screen

In the Middle Ages, a cathedral was used for many things in addition to public worship, and for this reason it was neces- sary to set aside a space exclusively for worship. In the Eng- lish cathedrals, a carved wooden screen called a rood screen traditionally separated the choir and altar from the nave. At Washington National Cathedral, the rood screen, a vestige of that tradition, has served less as a barrier and more as a mark- er, signifying the entry to the most sacred space in the build- ing and metaphorically into the kingdom of heaven. Now all major Cathedral services are held in the crossing, in front of the rood screen and fully in the midst of the congregation.

"Rood" is an Old English word for rod or pole and refers to the cross on which Jesus was crucified. This rood screen is made of carved oak. Under its delicate pointed arches, saints and religious symbols are carved into the wood. High above the rood screen is the rood beam with its surmount- ing crucifix. Mourning figures of Mary, the mother of Jesus, and John, the son of Zebedee, both of whom were present at the Crucifixion, flank the cross. A shield depicting the Lamb of God, a description of Jesus first used by John the Baptiz- er as a symbol of His sacrifice, is carved on the rood beam.

Each of the nine orders of angels are represented in the carvings in the stone soffit (the underside of the arch) above. Their ranking dates from the fifth century and refers to the hierarchy of angels who serve God in heaven. They are divided into groups by their roles: the Counselors, who surround the throne of God and have little contact with mortals, include the Seraphim, Cherubim, and Thrones; the Governors, who

represent the power of God and protect the human race, are the Dominions, Powers, and Virtues; and the Messengers, who are directly involved in human affairs, include the Prin- cipalities, Archangels, and Angels. In the north soffit, the carv- ings depict Angels, Principalities, Virtues, Thrones, and Seraphim. The carvings in the south represent Archangels, Powers, Dominions, and Cherubim.

The Jerusalem Cross

The crossing floor is inlaid with a Jerusalem Cross. Bishop Satterlee adopted this cross as the emblem of Washington National Cathedral. The large central cross represents the origins of Christianity in the Holy Land, while the small outer crosses stand for Christianity's reach to the four cor- ners of the earth. In its north arm, the Jerusalem Cross con- tains an emblem of St. Peter, the crossed keys of heaven traditionally vouchsafed by Jesus to Peter, and in its south arm, St. Paul's Sword of the Spirit (*spiritus gladius*), references to the apostle's letters and to his martyrdom. In the center is the monogram IHS, the first three letters from the Greek translation of Jesus' name. To complete the Trinity, the east and west branches of the cross contain the hand, symboliz- ing God the Father, and the dove, symbolizing the Holy Spir- it. The marble for the Cathedral floors was quarried in the state of Tennessee and in Italy.

To improve sightlines for worshipers, a substantial, yet portable, wooden platform sits over the Jerusalem Cross on the floor. The platform is also inlaid with a Jerusalem Cross, which is made from various types and colors of wood, and, while it covers the Cross on the floor, the wooden inlay mir- rors its design and placement.

THE ROSE WINDOWS

Among the most spectacular of the more than two hundred stained glass windows that illuminate the Cathedral are the three rose windows, which adorn the north and south transepts and the west end of the nave. Rose windows are a traditional and vital mode of artistic expression in Gothic cathedrals, and, unlike other stained glass windows, which generally observe a more literal and narrative style, they are often used to express a tenet of faith or a vision of God. The iconography of the three windows, *Creation* in the west, *Last Judgment* in the north, and *Church Triumphant* in the south, reflects humankind's birth, death, and redemption. The windows are fundamentally less about particular symbolic imagery, since details are difficult to read from floor level, than about the transcendent and ever-shifting quality of light and color they produce. The three rose windows were completed between 1932 and 1976, each the work of a different artist. The largest of the three, the north rose, is twenty-six feet in diameter. The most complex, the west rose, includes more than 10,500 pieces of glass.

Creation: The West Rose

Among the most memorable visual features in the Cathedral, the west rose window, entitled *Creation*, is one of very few abstract rose windows in the world. Set ablaze by the rays of the afternoon sun, the west rose celebrates God's formation of the universe. The abstractions unfold from the central white glass, which signifies the Word of God that sets Creation in motion, to ten radiating petals of paired lancets and from there to ten curvilinear multifoils interspersed with quatrefoils. The forms within the multifoils explore the majesty and mystery of Creation. These include abstract compositions inspired by the phases of the moon, the spiraling galaxies, the song of the birds, and, in the top multifoil, the four traditionally Greek elements (fire, air, earth, and water).

The window, which is almost twenty-six feet in diameter, was designed by Rowan LeCompte. Because the window is recessed more than fifteen feet into the façade, a large portion of the glass is in shadow half the day during many months of the year. To compensate for this, LeCompte used chipped nuggets of thick, colored glass that act like prisms, bending the sunlight into the interior. The colors

TRANSCENDENCE THROUGH COLOR AND LIGHT

One of the structural innovations that characterized Gothic architecture is the flying buttress, which served to counter the horizontal thrust of the pointed arches and vaulted ceilings. Consequently, the walls of Gothic cathedrals had less weight and did not need to be as massive. Less masonry allowed for larger and more numerous windows of colored glass.

The stained glass windows at Washington National Cathedral convey the color brilliance similar to that of the medieval period due to a technique of glass-making created by English glassblower William Edward Chance. In the late nineteenth century, Chance developed a process of making sheets of colored glass from mouth-blown cylinders.

The first stained glass windows made for Washington National Cathedral are in Bethlehem Chapel. Produced in London in 1912, the window's theme is the incarnation of Jesus Christ. In Neo-Gothic style, the stained glass is creat-ed with a fifteenth-century English technique of painting realistic details on white glass, resulting in muted tones of color. These windows are unlike any other in the Cathedral in that they diffuse rather than transmit the light.

A most unique combination of stained glass and stone tracery at Washington National Cathedral is the *Creation* window by Rowan LeCompte. It is unusual among rose windows because of its abstract design and its theme of creation. *Creation* is an abstract visualization from the Book of Genesis, "and the earth was without form and void and darkness was upon the face of the deep... and God said, 'Let there be light.'" Given that the window sits fifteen feet into the Cathedral's façade, LeCompte's ingenious use of large chunks of glass, which behave like prisms to bend light into the building, defied inherent shadows cast by the deep tracery and insured brilliance of color throughout the day.

Stained glass windows at Washington National Cathedral serve the same purpose as the stained glass windows of medieval times—telling biblical stories through pictures. The Cathedral windows are distinctively American in that they tell stories of the history of the Christian faith in the United States, as well as the history of other seekers of a spiritual life. These windows also highlight moments in American history and honor political, civic, and spiritual leaders from around the world.

change from moment to moment as the light shifts in accordance with the time of day, the season of the year, and the condition of the weather.

Describing his encounter with the splendor of the stained glass of the nave, Dieter Goldkuhle (b. 1938), who fabricated and installed *Creation*, among many other windows in the Cathedral, once said, "Arriving at the Cathedral in the early morning, I feel absolutely lost in dabs of color, in the abstract patterns the windows create on the piers. Even if you are not particularly religious, you must recognize this light as the physical presence of God."

Last Judgment: The North Rose

The north rose window represents the Last Judgment, a time foretold in the Gospels when Christ will sit in judgment of the world, separating the resurrected dead into the righteous and the damned. The window's design features more than seventy subjects, of which approximately two-thirds are figures and the rest symbols. At the center is Christ as Judge, seated on a throne, wearing a crown of gold and holding a scepter. Sixteen lancet windows emanating from the center depict angels, prophets from the Hebrew Bible, and figures from the parables of Jesus. The eight multifoils that encircle the lancets include scenes from the Book of Revelation and from the Gospel of Matthew. The open gates of heaven are visible in the top medallion, while the flames of hell wait at the bottom. The north rose window, the first of the three

✦ THE INTRICATELY
CARVED ARMRESTS IN THE
GREAT CHOIR VIVIDLY
BRING TO LIFE BIBLICAL
STORIES SUCH AS THAT OF
THE RAVENOUS WOLVES IN
SHEEPS' CLOTHING.

to be completed, is the work of Lawrence B. Saint (1885–1956), who also designed the three pairs of lancet windows beneath the rose window. These windows elaborate on the theme of the Last Judgment, with depictions of the prophets and saints of the Hebrew Bible and the New Testament.

Church Triumphant: The South Rose

Together, the north and south rose windows complete the story of Creation introduced in the west end. The south rose window's depiction of the Church Triumphant employs the imagery of the Book of Revelation. In the center medallion, God the Father sits upon his throne, wearing a golden mantle; he gives a blessing with his right hand and in his left he holds the Lamb of God, representing his son, the Christ. He is surrounded by the symbols for the four evangelists, Matthew, Mark, Luke, and John (human, lion, ox, and eagle). The petals of the rose represent the twenty-four elders, each holding a golden crown; the twelve outer medallions suggest the twelve gates of heaven guarded by angels. Apostles appear in the lancets below. This rose window was created by Joseph G. Reynolds, Jr. (1886–1972), and Wilbur H. Burnham (1887–1974).

THE HIGH ALTAR
AND THE GREAT CHOIR

The iconographic scheme and visual thrust of the entire main level of the Cathedral culminate in the High Altar, housed in the apse, or fourth arm, of the cruciform structure. The monumental scale of the High Altar reflects not only its liturgical significance, but also its need to be visible from the western portals one-tenth of a mile away. In fact, the cross behind the altar, which is made of wood, gilded brass, crystal, and enamel and stands nearly six feet tall, focuses the attention of the viewer, even from such a distance. The perception of distance is enhanced by a subtle and complex adjustment in the geometry of the Cathedral architecture that renders the *Majestus* slightly off-center. This is achieved by a subtle shift in the axis of the nave so that it does not exactly match that of the apse: it is not a straight line from the center of the central portal in the west to the center of the *Majestus* in the east. This adjustment in the axis for aesthetic purposes causes the crossing to be "out of square."

The High Altar is referred to as the Jerusalem Altar because it is made of limestone from an ancient quarry out-side Jerusalem, from where, it is believed, came the stone used to build King Solomon's temple. The altar is freestanding so that the priest may face the congregation during the celebration of the sacrament of Holy Communion. Ten stones representing the Ten Commandments are set into the floor directly in front of the altar. The six-inch-square stones were brought to the Cathedral from the Chapel of Moses on Mount Sinai. A needlepoint rug in colors that reflect the surrounding marble covers the stones.

The needlepoint around the High Altar is purposefully designed with great clarity and bright colors to be effectively viewed from a distance. The long rug leading up the steps to the altar is a prime example. It was designed by the Misses Tebbetts, four sisters from Kent, Connecticut, who were outstanding designers of church embroidery and needlepoint for more than fifty years. The finished rug is twenty-one feet by nine feet, and was worked on a ten-mesh canvas in twenty-two separate pieces. Although twenty-three people stitched the rug, it was assembled and joined by a single person with such craftsmanship that the seams are virtually invisible.

The High Altar Reredos

The wall behind the High Altar is entitled the *Ter Sanctus* (thrice holy) reredos. It sets forth in richly carved stone the hymn sung during the Eucharistic liturgy: "Therefore with angels and archangels and with all the company of heaven, we laud and magnify thy glorious name." The 110 carved figures that surround the *Majestus* represent saints, prophets, and martyrs whose lives exemplify the highest ideals of Christianity, as well as angels, who praise God. Six anonymous figures, three on each side of the center panel, allude to the six-fold test articulated in the Gospel of Matthew: "For I was hungry and you gave me food, I was thirsty and you gave me something to drink, I was a stranger and you welcomed me, I was naked and you gave me clothing, I was sick and you took care of me, I was in prison and you visited me." The six figures represent all those whose works embody these ideals, and invite each of us to perform these charitable acts in daily life.

The reredos is carved from French Caen stone. The fine grain and greater luminosity of this stone differs from that used elsewhere in

✦ WHEN CONSTRUCTION
WAS BEGUN ON THIS POR-
TION OF THE CATHEDRAL
IN 1915, AN AMERICAN
FLAG WAS RAISED EACH
MORNING ABOVE THE
SITE, TO REMAIN THERE
UNTIL CONSTRUCTION
WAS COMPLETED.

the Cathedral, allowing for more detail in the carving and contrast in brightness. The screen was carved by Hilgartner Marble Company of Baltimore, Maryland. The figures are the work of sculptor Angelo Lualdi (1881–1979).

The Majestus

The centerpiece of the reredos and the focus of the iconographic design of the Cathedral is the figure of Christ in Majesty. This image of Christ is shown with his right hand raised in a gesture of blessing and his left hand holding a globe that is topped by a cross, which signifies his sovereignty over the entire world. The Texas limestone from which the *Majestus* is carved is brighter still in tone than the French Caen stone that surrounds it. The model for the *Majestus* design, by sculptor Walker Hancock (1901–1998), was approved in 1967. Rendered by master stone carver Roger Morigi and his associate Frank Zic (1907–1995), the sculpture took two years to complete.

The Apse Windows

Three windows of brilliantly colored glass occupy a position of honor directly above the High Altar. They depict events crucial to the Christian belief: Christ's reign in Majesty (cen-ter), His Crucifixion (north), and His Resurrection (south). All three windows were created by Joseph G. Reynolds, Jr., and Wilbur H. Burnham. In color harmony and palette, these windows are modeled after those in the Cathedral of Santa Maria de Regla in León, Spain, a decision promoted by James Sheldon, a stained glass expert, member of the Cathedral's Building Committee, and friend and benefactor of the Cathedral for many years. Upon their completion, Sheldon declared that the apse windows could be "likened to a hymn of exaltation played upon the instrument of color." Flanking these in the north and south are two additional clerestory windows, designed by Rowan LeCompte, which complement the central trio with depictions of the childhood of Jesus (north) and his Transfiguration as the Christ (south). With these, LeCompte sought to convey the richness of the Christian story, which asserts both the humanity and the divinity of Christ.

Above the *Ter Sanctus* reredos, in the friezes on the walls beneath the triforium gallery, are carved verses from the ancient hymn, *Te Deum Laudamus* (*We Praise Thee O*

God), which is often sung at Morning Prayer and as a hymn of thankfulness on special occasions. A pair of sixty-five-feet tall stained glass windows (three tiers of two lancets), invisible from the nave, are incorporated into the north and south walls of the apse. Intended to ensure that the High Altar is the most brightly illuminated space in the Cathedral, they illustrate additional verses from the *Te*

Deum. The lancets of the south wall are inscribed: "The Holy Church throughout the world doth acknowledge Thee." The lancets in the north wall depict another verse: "The noble army of martyrs praise Thee." This pair of windows, the tallest in the Cathedral, was created by Earl Edward Sanborn (1890–1937). His designs are distinguished by the extensive use of transparent, or "white," glass. This

GIVING PRAISE THROUGH MUSIC

Music is the heart of the liturgical life of the Cathedral. This is reflected in the history of the music program and in the central location of the choir and the great organ in their beautifully carved oak quarters. On September 29, 1907, a combined choir of men and boys from St. Paul's K Street, St. John's Lafayette Square, St. John's Georgetown Parish, and St. Mark's Capitol Hill sang, accompanied by the United States Marine Band, for the ceremonial laying of the Cathedral's Foundation Stone. In the many years since, the purpose of the Cathedral choirs has been to offer, at the highest standard possible, praises to God through leadership in music and liturgy. The Cathedral Choir of Men and Boys was founded in 1909 and the Cathedral Choir of Men and Girls in 1997. The girl and boy choristers are

scholarship students at the Cathedral schools; the choirmen are professional singers based in the Washington/Baltimore metropolitan area. Services include a choral evensong Monday through Thursday and on Sundays; on major festival days, a full choral Eucharist and choral evensong are sung. Throughout the year, the Cathedral musicians and diverse guest artists present numerous recitals and concerts of both sacred and secular music at the Cathedral.

In keeping with the tradition of expanding musical offerings at the Cathedral, a mixed-voice, adult choir has been formed. Cathedral Voices, a choir of forty volunteer singers and eight professional section leaders, sings for the early morning Eucharist held in the nave each Sunday.

✤ *CATHEDRAL BENEFACTOR BESSIE KIBBEY DONATED $500 IN 1901 TO COMMISSION A CATHEDRA MADE PARTIALLY FROM TWENTY-THREE GLASTONBURY ABBEY STONES.*

feature and the windows' great height maximize the daylight cast into the sanctuary.

The Communion Rail

The oak communion rail, which separates the chancel from the sanctuary, is supported by twelve posts. Eleven of these posts bear the carved likenesses of each of the eleven apostles. At the northernmost end of the rail, a twelfth post, representing Judas Iscariot, the betrayer of Jesus, has been left uncarved in token of his unfinished character. The needlepoint kneeling cushions at the base of the rail feature motifs symbolic of the Eucharist (sprays of wheat and clusters of grapes), the Passion (the crown of thorns and spear), and the Resurrection of Jesus Christ (the crown of glory and butterflies).

The Glastonbury Cathedra

Cathedra means "bishop's chair" and is the word from which cathedral, "the place of the bishop," is derived. Washington National Cathedral is the seat of the Episcopal Bishop of Washington and the seat of the Presiding Bishop of the Episcopal Church of the United States (ECUSA). On the north side of the sanctuary is the Glastonbury Cathedra, a large chair fabricated of stones from the ancient

Glastonbury Abbey in England. Tradition holds that the church at Glastonbury was founded by St. Joseph of Arimathea in about 43 CE, several hundred years before Augustine and his missionaries arrived in Britain. The Glastonbury Cathedra symbolizes the continuity of the Church and the tie between the Church of England and the Episcopal Church in the United States. In 1990, the Archbishop of Canterbury witnessed the setting of a compass rose in the marble floor directly in front of the Glastonbury Cathedra. The points of the compass symbolize the worldwide dimensions of the Anglican Communion.

The Sedilia

In the south wall of the sanctuary, to the right as you face the High Altar, are three seats set into canopied niches. This traditional sanctuary furnishing, called the sedilia, is used by priests taking part in services. Distinguished visitors and members of the Cathedral Chapter and of the Foundation's Board of Trustees also sit in the sedilia. The finials of the pointed arches carry carved figures of three outstanding priests of the church and writers: Howard Thurman (1900–1981), John Donne (1572–1631), and George Herbert (1593–1633). These three statues, created by sculptor

INTRICACIES IN IRON

Samuel Yellin (1885–1940), the foremost American iron craftsman of the twentieth century, designed and installed ironwork at the Cathedral from 1925 to 1940. Each of Yellin's gates and grilles for the nave-level chapels is decorated with symbols representative of each chapel's theme: for St. Mary's Chapel, the rose, the five-pointed star, the fleur-de-lis, and the letter "M"; in St. John's Chapel, the eagle and a cup with an emerging viper; for Children's Chapel, whimsical flora and fauna; and in the War Memorial Chapel, crenellation resembling the protective battlements of medieval castles. Yellin, who described his craft as the "salt and pepper of architecture," considered the iron gates and grilles he created for St. Mary's Chapel in 1934 to be his finest work, "a wrought iron grille and gates of surpassing beauty in design."

Chas Fagan (b. 1966), are among the most recent additions to the fabric of the Cathedral.

The Great Choir

The long stalls of the Great Choir stand between the sanctuary and the nave. The stalls were designed by the Cathedral architects and intricately carved from oak by furniture makers Irving & Casson-A.H. Davenport and Company. The stalls provide seats for the congregation during daily services, and for the Cathedral choir and visiting singers during Sunday services. On occasion, an audience for intimate chamber music concerts occupies them. Distinguished visitors, canons, and the members of the Cathedral Chapter use these seats, also. The choir stalls are furnished with needlepoint cushions on which are stitched the seals of all the dioceses and missionary districts of the Episcopal Church. Other seat cushions feature depictions of liturgical music and music instruments noted in the Bible, such as horns, flutes, harps, bells, and cymbals.

Two canopied choir seats at the altar end of the choir are reserved for the Presiding Bishop of the Episcopal Church of the United States (ECUSA), on the north, and the Bishop of Washington, on the south. The stall set aside for the Bishop of Washington is distinguished by a carving depicting the consecration of Thomas John Claggett (1743–1816), the first Episcopal Bishop of Maryland and the first bishop to be consecrated on American soil. The two small figures in the

canopy over this stall are William Croswell Doane (1832–1913), first Bishop of Albany, and Henry Yates Satterlee (1843–1908), first Bishop of Washington. Among numerous other choir seats designated for the use of various dignitaries associated with the Cathedral and the Cathedral schools are stalls marked with the respective seals of the Chaplains of the U.S. Senate and House of Representatives, and reserved for their use. The clergy stalls at the nave end of the choir are used by the dean, Cathedral canons, and visiting preachers during services.

Each of the armrests on the choir stalls bears a uniquely carved image. The designs include Noah's Ark, Moses in the bulrushes, the angel appearing to the shepherds on Christmas Eve, and various Christian symbols, such as the pelican, the fish, and the unicorn. Although the carvers worked from a general plan and were guided by the traditional aesthetics of the English Gothic style, they imprinted their own twentieth-century and particularly American point of view onto numerous carvings, for example, with the appearance of finials in the shape of cornstalks where medieval tradition would have suggested acanthus leaves. A striking record of the Second World War era during which the stalls were carved: The armrest of one of the stalls fea-

✣ THE CATHEDRAL IS CURRENTLY PLANNING ON INSTALLING TWO NEW ORGANS, ONE IN THE EAST END AND ANOTHER IN THE WEST GALLERY, TO BETTER SUPPORT THE LITURGY AND CONGREGATIONAL SINGING.

The vision of the Cathedral founders for a great church in the nation's capital still guides us. Today this magnificent, transcendent space welcomes all people and proclaims the power of God's love to change our lives and our world.

—JOHN B. CHANE
Bishop of Washington

tures a carved lion, the symbol of Britain, devouring a snake whose head is a caricature of Adolf Hitler. The subtlety with which this sort of detail is executed adds richness and humanity to the construction of the Great Choir without disturbing its formal harmony.

The first pipe organ for the Cathedral was the work of Ernest M. Skinner, America's foremost organ artisan of the early twentieth century. A pioneer who perfected electro-pneumatic key action, grandeur of tone, and lush orchestral colors, Skinner first supplied an instrument for Bethlehem Chapel in 1912, then a temporary organ in 1932 for use in the completed choir.

The Great Organ was completed in 1938 by the Ernest M. Skinner and Son Organ Company to specifications developed with Cathedral organists Edgar Priest (1878–1935) and Robert G. Barrows (1911–1987) and with other technical experts. Cathedral architects, along with furniture maker Irving & Casson-A.H. Davenport and Company, designed and built the elaborately carved case-fronts. Each case contains forty-four speaking pipes. Unlike almost every other pipe organ, however, these cases do not actually contain the instrument: the remaining eight-thousand-odd pipes were installed in specially prepared chambers at the triforium level, with the largest bass pipes disposed horizontally.

Changes and additions to the organ since its installation reflect the increasing size of the Cathedral itself as construction continued, as well as an evolving musical taste. In 1958, Aeolian-Skinner (Skinner's successor firm) provided a new console, unique at the time for its hydraulically height-adjustable pedal board, which was designed to accommodate the contrast in physical stature between organists Paul Callaway (1909–1995) and Richard Wayne Dirksen (1921–2003). As for the rest of the organ, large-scale transformative plans established in 1957 were accomplished in various stages through 1975. In 1965, the commanding *Trompette en Chamade* was installed in the eastern-most triforium above the *Majestus*, where it remains a musical and visual fixture.

THE NAVE CHAPELS

Five chapels surround the sanctuary and choir. The two chapels closest to the sanctuary mirror the traditional presentation in Christian art of Mary, the mother of Jesus, on the left of the cross, and John, his devoted apostle and evangelist, on the right. The inclusion of Holy Spirit Chapel with the other nave chapels asserts the Christian belief in the Trinity, the three persons of God—Father, Son, and Holy Spirit. The remaining two chapels, the Children's Chapel and the War Memorial Chapel, underscore the important concerns of the Cathedral builders, namely, honoring the spiritual lives of children and the men and women of the United States who serve in defense of their country.

Holy Spirit Chapel

Situated just beyond the north transept aisle, adjacent to the parclose stairway, Holy Spirit Chapel is set aside for private prayer and meditation. In its small quarters are arrayed many exquisite examples of the liturgical arts that are found throughout the Cathedral. This beloved chapel is, in a sense, a microcosm of the larger Cathedral.

The reredos, in the form of a painted triptych elaborately framed in oak carvings by Irving & Casson-A.H. Davenport and Company, presents a serene vision of heaven and the descent of the Holy Spirit. The painted oak panels, completed in 1936, are the work of noted American illustrator and painter

✥ *"I WISH VERY DEEPLY THAT THIS FIGURE OF CHRIST, AND THE SURROUNDING EMBELLISHMENTS, BE SIGNIFICANT TO THE MODERN WORSHIPER, AND NOT A MUSEUM PIECE."*
—ANDREW WYETH, 1934

who designed and installed ironwork at the Cathedral from 1925
to 1940.

The single stained glass window, created by Nicola D'Ascenzo
(1871–1954), that lights the chapel
depicts the meeting of Jesus and the
woman of Samaria at the well. The
colors in the glass are inspired by
fire, a further reference to the Holy
Spirit, who is symbolized by a flame.

St. Mary's Chapel

Imposing wrought iron gates,
designed and fabricated by Samuel
Yellin, serve a purpose similar to
that of the rood screen, creating a
sacred enclosure housing the four
remaining chapels on the main
level of the Cathedral. The gates
extend from the rood screen at
the west end of the Great Choir
and separate the apse from the
nave and transepts. Gates in the north transept, near Holy
Spirit Chapel, lead to a chapel dedicated to Mary, the mother of Jesus.

The altar of St. Mary's Chapel lies just north of the
Cathedral's High Altar. The gilded and polychromed altar
reredos is carved of linden wood and depicts significant
moments in Mary's life. The reredos is another of the wood-
en masterpieces in the Cathedral by Irving & Casson-A.H.
Davenport and Company. The panels on the upper left and
right depict the Annunciation and Mary's visit to Elizabeth,
respectively. In the two center scenes, Mary is shown holding the Christ Child in her hands as she presents him to the
world, and standing in grief at the foot of the cross. In the
lower right and left are scenes of the marriage in Cana of
Galilee, when Mary witnessed Jesus' first miracle, and the
upper room on the day of Pentecost, where Mary gathered
with the disciples.

Following medieval custom, the donors of the chapel,
Larz and Isabel Anderson, are represented by two tiny kneel-
ing figures in the lower left and right corners of the reredos.
Anderson, an American diplomat and veteran of the Span-

❖❖ *A SMALL FIGURE OF*
ST. JOSEPH STANDS ABOVE
THE SACRISTY DOOR, TO
THE RIGHT OF THE
LINDEN WOOD REREDOS
IN ST. MARY'S CHAPEL.

N.C. Wyeth (1882–1945). Surrounding the radiant central figure of the ascended Christ are
the angels of the heavenly host
praising the Lord with voice
and instruments. The dove, an
ancient symbol of the Holy Spirit, unites the remaining
iconography of the chapel. Doves appearing in the seven
panels, which form the predella of the reredos, allude to the
seven gifts of the Holy Spirit found in the words of Isaiah.
In this scripture the prophet foretells the coming of a Messiah and the wisdom of God (seven gifts) he will possess:
"But a shoot shall sprout from the stump of Jesse, and from
his roots a bud shall blossom. The spirit of the Lord shall
rest upon him: a spirit of wisdom and of understanding, a
spirit of counsel and of strength, a spirit of knowledge and
of fear of the Lord, and his delight shall be the fear of the
Lord." The dove motif is repeated in the wrought iron
gates and grilles that enclose Holy Spirit Chapel. These
are among the masterworks of the foremost artist black-
smith of the twentieth century, Samuel Yellin (1885–1940),

✤ *The tapestries in St. Mary's Chapel portray the bravery of David, the shepherd boy who became a king, as he fought and killed the giant Goliath.*

The Main Level

ish-American War, and his wife Isabel are interred in the carved tomb on the north wall of the chapel. In memory of her husband, Isabel Anderson bestowed on the Cathedral six sixteenth-century Flemish tapestries that are among the many treasures in the collection of the Cathedral. Woven in Milan by Flemish weavers, these tapestries were originally purchased by Count d'Estes as a wedding gift. Adorning the side walls of the chapel and a wall of Holy Spirit Chapel, these exquisite works record scenes from the life of David, in particular, his encounter with Goliath. The shade of blue in the tapestries is repeated in the background of the needle-point kneelers, which feature Mary's monogram and other Marian symbols.

Other decorative elements of the chapel depart from the primary theme of the life of Mary. The stained glass windows depict the parables Jesus used to teach moral truths. Designed and fabricated by Lawrence Saint, the windows feature images from the Good Samaritan, the Prodigal Son, the Sower, the Ten Virgins, and other narratives from the Gospels of the New Testament. For these three windows, as well as for the four in St. John's Chapel that illustrate Jesus' miracles, Saint made the choice to use living models to render the figures in the windows. For the Good Samaritan, he selected a man well-known for his benevolent nature; for the disciples, he enlisted fishermen from the coast of New Jersey; and for his depiction of Lazarus, he studied the pain-worn visage of an invalid.

Overhead, the vaulting bosses represent the seven sacraments of the Church: baptism, confirmation, matrimony, holy orders, penance, unction of the sick (anointing with oil), and Holy Communion.

THE NATION'S CHURCH

The War Memorial Chapel, with its many representations of suffering, valor, and patriotism, is only one expression of the national significance of the Cathedral Church of St. Peter and St. Paul. At the entrance to the Cathedral, the floor of the Narthex includes a mosaic of the seals of each of the fifty states and the District of Columbia, surrounding the Great Seal of the United States. Memorials for George Washington and Abraham Lincoln and the tomb of Woodrow Wilson pay tribute to these honored presidents of the United States.

Several stained glass windows present the American theme. The first window of the south arcade (progressing from the west) is *Founding of a New Nation,* an abstract design symbolizing the search for freedom that led to the founding of America. This window was dedicated in 1976, as America celebrated its second centennial. Opposing this window in the north arcade is *Agony of Civil War*. Here, the horror of civil war is given physical expression in the use of blood reds and smoky grays of cannon fire. In the north outer aisle, *America the Beautiful I* and *America the Beautiful II* adorn the Bettelheim Bay, with notes of freshness and variety. Artists Rowan and Irene LeCompte capture the complexity of unifying cultural images through use of symbolic colors: blossoms of southern orchards; the great red rocks of the Southwest; burning skies of western deserts; waves of grain and open skies of the Midwestern plains; and autumn leaves and wintry forests of the northern states.

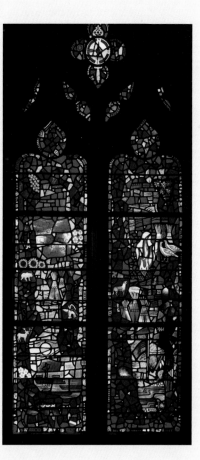

✦ *THE HEAD OF THE*
CRUCIFIED CHRIST,
A DETAIL FROM THE
REREDOS IN
ST. JOHN'S CHAPEL

St. John's Chapel

To the right of the sanctuary is the chapel dedicated to St. John. The reredos, which is carved directly into the surface of the chapel wall, portrays the Crucifixion, with the vigil of Mary, the mother of Jesus, on the right of the cross, and John, his devoted apostle and evangelist, on the left. Below the cross is a bas-relief of the Last Supper in which John is seated next to Jesus. In the left corners of the reredos are the figures of James, John's brother, and Zebedee, his father. In the right corners are Polycarp, Bishop of Smyrna, who was John's favorite pupil, and Mary Salome, John's mother. The needlework of the kneelers around the altar incorporates imagery from the Book of Revelation, attributed to St. John. The designs include the eagle, which symbolizes the soaring and revelatory quality of John's gospel. Carved boss stones in the vaulting above St. John's Chapel represent the seven gifts of the Holy Spirit.

A recessed area in the south wall of the chapel frames the tomb and statue of Norman Prince (1887–1916), a young aviator who distinguished himself in aerial combat over France during World War I. At the outbreak of the war, before the United States entered the conflict, Prince was determined to serve the Allied cause and was among the founding members of the *Escadrille Américaine,* later known as the Lafayette Escadrille, a squadron of American pilots who flew as volunteers for France. Prince died following a failed landing attempt on October 15, 1916. He was originally buried in France, but in 1937 was reinterred at the Cathedral upon the request of his parents, Frederick H. and Abigail Prince, early Cathedral benefactors who provided the funds for the building of the chapel. Both the statue and the tomb are the work of Paul Landowski (1875–1961).

The stained glass of four two-lancet windows found here portrays twenty-five of the miracles performed by Jesus, as recorded by the four evangelists in the New Testament. They are illustrated in medallions, differently shaped in each window, and framed by delicate patterns of leaves and flowers. Lawrence Saint designed these windows, as well as eleven others for the Cathedral.

✦ *WITH A HIGHLY*
DEVELOPED GEOMETRIC
TRACERIED BACKGROUND,
THE REREDOS IN ST. JOHN'S
CHAPEL OFFERS A WEALTH
OF LACE-LIKE CARVING
IN LIMESTONE.

Though not a part of the biblical iconography of the chapel, the kneeling cushions provided with the congregational seating are among the best-known of the more than 1,500 works of needlepoint in the Cathedral. These kneelers commemorate men and women who have made significant contributions to American history, including 39 U.S. presidents. Each kneeler uses symbols to recount the individual's accomplishments: a violin and a scientific equation characterize Albert Einstein; a ship, an anchor, and a great white whale represent Herman Melville; a rocket, commemorating the beginning of the U.S. space program, is among the symbols for John F. Kennedy; and a ballot box and quill pen signify Susan B. Anthony's crusade for women's rights. The kneelers are constantly in rotation, for conservation and maintenance purposes, and new kneelers are occasionally added.

Children's Chapel

Although it has become customary in many houses of worship to set aside special places for children, such as a children's corner or a children's arch, only one other cathedral is known to have set aside a chapel for the use of children. Parents who were Cathedral benefactors donated the funds for this chapel in memory of their own son, who lived for only six years.

The theme of the chapel unfolds near its entrance, where a bronze statue of a boy, his arms flung wide in welcome, greets all who enter. The sculpture, entitled *The Child Jesus,* is the work of Mary Aldrich Fraser (1884–1967). Entrance gates by Samuel Yellin signal a playful and imaginative tone, with fanciful flowers and the whimsical heads of birds and other animals. Inside, the fan vaulting of the ceiling of the chapel is deliberately lowered to enable a close view of its elaborate carving. Indeed, all the furnishings of this chapel, including the reredos, baptismal font, altar,

chairs, even the pipe organ, are scaled to accommodate the size of a six-year-old child. References to children in the Bible abound. The stained glass window, designed by George Gugert (d. 1958), tells the stories of Samuel and David as boys. The gilt reredos, of carved wood, features on the lower left the young Jesus confounding the elders in the temple and, on the right, Jesus saying, "Suffer the little children to come unto me." Even the needlepoint kneelers in this small chapel are made with an eye to delight children. Designs of baby animals of all kinds are featured, including those on the communion kneeler preparing to enter Noah's Ark.

The small figures above the altar panels are Peter and Paul, patron saints of the Cathedral, while in the center of the reredos is the risen Christ with his mother Mary on his right and John, the beloved disciple, on his left. In the wall to the left of the altar, a statue by Hazel Clere of St. Michael slaying the dragon symbolizes the power of good to overcome evil. According to tradition, St. Michael is the prince

✤ CHILDREN'S CHAPEL PROVIDES A CHARMING SANCTUARY FOR SMALL AND BIG PEOPLE, ALIKE, FOR ALL THOSE WHO SEEK THE SIMPLICITY OF A CHILD'S FAITH.

of guardian angels, a reminder of the psalmist's words that God "shall give his angels charge over thee, and keep thee in all thy ways." Another carving, depicting John the Baptizer as a young boy, appears in the wall above the grille openings of the chapel's north wall.

War Memorial Chapel

A powerful sculpture of the suffering Christ installed above the altar signals the theme of the War Memorial Chapel. This work, by British artist Steven Sykes (1914–1999), features the dramatically oversized head of the crucified Redeemer crowned with a halo of brass shapes simulating canon shells, and irregular rays of cast aluminum suggesting the rays of glory. With this image as its focal point, the chapel recognizes the suffering of war and honors the men and women who have dedicated their lives to their country through service in the Armed Forces. Though the architects' original plans did not call for a chapel in the south transept, such a space seemed necessary and appropriate after World War II.

Members of America's Armed Forces have come to regard this chapel as their special place in the Cathedral. In the bookcases to the right of the altar is a National Roll of Honor containing the names and dates of service of thousands of military men and women who have served their country. The bookcases are decorated with the service ribbons of the five branches of the Armed Forces.

The nine-foot by twelve-foot needlepoint hanging on the east wall of the chapel uses the biblical symbol of the Tree of Life to not only honor the armed services but also to illustrate the expansion of the United States. Emblems of the Armed Forces and the Great Seal of the United States surround the tree. Seals of each of the fifty states and the District of Columbia appear in the order in which the states joined the Union, with the thirteen original colonies in the lowest branches and Alaska and Hawaii at the top. The border of twining ivy symbolizes the fidelity of all the valiant defenders of this country. White crosses at the bottom honor those who have died in battle.

The three Freedom windows in the chapel honor those from biblical times to the mid-twentieth century who gave their lives for the cause of freedom. These richly colored and glowing windows depict many significant historical events in that struggle, from the supreme sacrifice of Christ upon the cross in the central window over the altar, to the sacrifices of those who fought in World War II. Joseph G. Reynolds, Jr., created these windows in 1952 and 1953.

Additional facets of the chapel's decoration honor ties between Great Britain and the United States. The original needlepoint kneelers of various abstract geometric designs were stitched by British women (including one stitched by Her Majesty Queen Elizabeth The Queen Mother) in thanksgiving for America's assistance during World War II. Carved on the communion rail, in further acknowledgment of the

In 1982, during a three-day healing vigil, the names of the 57,939 Americans who died in the Vietnam war were read in War Memorial Chapel.

relationship, is a small statue of St. George, patron saint of England. The statue was carved by Herbert Read (d. 1972) of St. Sidwell's Art Works, Exeter, England.

The north boundary of the War Memorial Chapel is marked by waist-high carved oak screens given by the Twenty-eighth Marine Regiment on the twentieth anniversary of the battle of Iwo Jima. A more recent addition to chapel furnishings is the Pentagon Memorial Cross, donated by the chaplains of the United States Army to honor those who died in the terrorist attack of September 11, 2001, and those who helped in the rescue effort. Presented after the daily evensong on December 2, 2003, the cross is one of four crosses created from the rubble of the Pentagon façade by Alvin

Neider, an artist and stone mason. The Cross has an intentionally unfinished appearance.

THE TRANSEPTS
The South Transept and the Baptistery
Facing the High Altar from the crossing, the south transept is the right arm of the Cathedral. The ceiling beneath the balcony is polychromed with a blue-green and gold pattern based on the Jerusalem Cross. This ornamentation recalls the medieval tradition of colorful interiors in cathedrals, which tradition was supplanted in the nineteenth and twentieth centuries by a preference for unadorned stone. The south portal

BEAUTY IN THE DETAILS

Since the Cathedral's inception, the Altar Guild and the Flower Guild of Washington National Cathedral have provided support for the ongoing preparation of 1,500 regularly scheduled worship services during the year. More than 150 volunteers offer their time and skill preparing for weekly services, weddings, funerals, and other important events. The Guild, under the leadership of the Flower and Altar Guild coordinator, is responsible for overseeing all flower arrangements throughout the Cathedral and the upkeep of all brass and silver altar furnishings and altar linens. The group keeps every service at the Cathedral in tune with the appropriate mood for the time of the church year with immaculate settings and flower arrangements that range from the sparseness of the Lenten Season to the abundant joy of Eastertide.

In 1996, the Flower Guild was the first group associated with a religious institution to be invited to the prestigious, by-invitation-only Philadelphia Flower Show, and since then has been invited twice more. The Cathedral's award-winning guild hosts two annual weeklong workshops at the Cathedral, attended by flower arrangers from around the world. Also, guild members travel to conferences across the U.S., giving flower arrangement demonstrations and workshops.

✤ *A wrought-iron bishop decorates one of master ironworker Jacob Schmidt's elaborate hinges.*

is framed on the interior with carved oak screening. On the exterior, each pair of massive wooden doors bears ten elaborately wrought iron hinges, the final project of Jacob Schmidt (d. 1964), one of the most gifted craftspeople in Samuel Yellin's Philadelphia studio and one of his successors at the Cathedral.

The twenty-six bosses in the high vaulting of the south transept, modeled by sculptor Heinz Warneke (1895–1983), refer to the office of Morning Prayer from the Book of Common Prayer. Specifically, the carvings illustrate the canticle *Benedicite, omnia opera Domini,* "Oh all ye works of the Lord, bless ye the Lord, praise Him and magnify Him forever."

In the west aisle of the south transept is the baptistery of the Cathedral. The font, carved of pink Tennessee marble and set upon a raised marble base, is set into the transept floor. Its decorative embellishments feature symbols of the sacrament of Baptism, such as scallop shells, waves of water, fishes, and the dove. Its peripheral location reflects the custom of the Church in the early twentieth century. Today, however, the sacrament of baptism has been re-emphasized and a baptismal font is often placed in the mid-nave crossing.

✤ *During the Advent season, the Cathedral's crèche, carved by sculptor Barbara Hughes, is placed in front of the baptismal font, awaiting the coming of the Baby Jesus*

In the baptistery, as elsewhere in the Cathedral, an iconographic theme unifies the decorative elements. Above the font, to the south and to the west, a pair of three-lancet windows, the work of Wilbur H. Burnham, portrays events associated with baptism. The theme of the window in the south wall is the theology of baptism, with the baptism of Jesus as its central image; the surrounding medallions represent the principle parts of the Anglican ministration of Holy Baptism. In the west wall, the window narrates the history of baptism, which begins with Jesus' commandment to his disciples, "Go ye into all the world and baptize," extending to representations of baptism throughout Christian history. Symbols of baptism, including shells and water motifs, appear in the borders of both windows.

The carved bosses in the vaulting overhead depict the ministration of baptism through scenes and symbols. The large bosses portray missionaries among people of different nations; the smaller bosses illustrate the Christian faith embracing the diversity of the human race through the sacrament of baptism. The baptismal symbol of the scallop shell is repeated on the needlepoint cushions on the bench along the wall.

An additional window in the west wall of the transept departs from the theme of baptism but merits notice nonetheless. It is believed to be the only publicly displayed window in the United States by Evie Hone (1894–1955), a stained glass artist of Irish birth whose renown rests on the expressive intensity of her style. Installed in 1953, it is the first in the Cathedral to be designed and installed by a woman. In its evocation of the healing grace of Jesus, the window marks a stylistic shift in the stained glass windows of the Cathedral toward freer design, richer hues, and brighter effects of light.

✤ *Looking across the crossing, from the north transept balcony to the south transept*

The North Transept

The north transept is the arm of the Cathedral to the left of the crossing. In the northwest corner is a cenotaph honoring James E. Freeman, third Bishop of Washington (1923–1943). His memorial of Indiana limestone bears a recumbent effigy of the bishop designed

and executed by Bryant Baker (1881–1970). A carved open book lies at the feet of the effigy: on one page is a representation of the tower entrance of the Cathedral College and on the other is the façade of the north transept. Bishop Freeman was responsible for raising the financial means to build both structures. An energetic and determined fundraiser, Freeman traveled by train all around the country, sometimes scheduling five or more events in a day, working long hours to raise money for the completion of the Cathedral, which he optimistically believed could be accomplished in five years. During his twenty years of dedicated leadership at the Cathedral, Bishop Freeman oversaw the completion of the choir and apse, the three main crypt chapels, the north transept, and St. Mary's, St. John's, and the Children's Chapels.

The wrought iron gate that forms the entrance to the balcony stairs is the work of Jacob Schmidt. A small lancet window, visible through the arch, depicts the biblical story of Jacob's vision of a ladder reaching up to heaven, with angels descending and ascending.

The exterior doors of the north transept open into an

A CATHEDRAL FOR ALL PEOPLE

Washington National Cathedral is a visual beacon of spirituality in Washington, D.C., and, through its many programs of inspiration, education, and outreach, serves as a place that nurtures and empowers all people. This function is reflected in the artwork throughout the awe-inspiring structure, as well as through its many programs.

The many niche figures throughout the Cathedral represent not only leaders in the Christian faith, but leaders associated with other faiths and the secular world. Niche statues of Dionysus of Greece and Kagawa of Japan decorate the Bettelheim Bay. In the Humanitarian Bay, two of the six figures of leaders who fostered furthering human rights are portrayed in the stained glass windows: Elizabeth of Hungary and George Washington Carver; carved figures and saints, such as Albert Schweitzer and Sir Wilfred Grenfell, appear on the corbels; and the niche statues are of St. Olaf of Norway and St. Francis of Assisi. The "Philosophers" stained glass window depicts humanity's search for knowledge as it moves from the merely rational to the discernment of truth through revelation.

A unique blend of the spiritual and the civic, this Gothic cathedral is a twenty-first century voice for generous-spirited Christianity and a catalyst for interfaith dialogue, in order to create a more hopeful and just world. Reflecting this mission during our centennial year, the Cathedral hosted Pray for Peace Benefit Concert and Prayer Ceremony, the Martin Luther King Day Celebration of Youth Non-Violence, and Breakthrough: The Women, Faith, and Development Summit to End Global Poverty. Supporting these and other events, the Cathedral College offers lectures, courses, and continuing education opportunities. And the

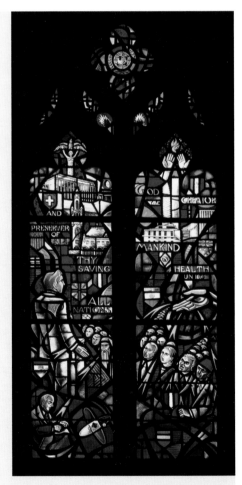

weekly Sunday Forum, hosted by Dean Samuel T. Lloyd III between morning services, has attracted thousands (in person and on the Web) seeking lively and thoughtful discussions of the critical issues of the day in the light of faith.

intimate vestibule of carved English oak and copper-framed clear glazing made by St. Sidwell's Art Works, England. The concrete ceiling above this entrance, like its counterpart in the south transept, is colorfully polychromed, here in red and gold. In 1986, when the ceiling was being painted, the orbit of Halley's comet was visible. The artist, Carl Tucker (b. 1920), indulged his enthusiasm for the meteorological event by adding the image of a comet to the otherwise formal and geometric design. The subsequent comment of a passerby—"What, a comet and no stars?"—prompted Tucker to add a star.

The walls of the north transept also bear notes of humor with which its creators garnished the Cathedral fabric. To the left of the gateway leading to the north balcony steps are tiny stone carvings of three church mice and their natural enemy, the cat. A rib of tracery symbolically separates these creatures, insurance against the legend that when the cat catches the last mouse, the Cathedral will fall. To the right of the north transept entrance is the door into the slype, or clergy robing room. The label mould terminations on each side of the door are carved with cannons, a visual pun referring to the Cathedral canons, or clergy, who use the room for vesting. Each termination's sculpture has a stack of books, symbolic of the hymnals and prayer books that canons must carry to and from services. Throughout the building, such spontaneous and lighthearted flourishes record the personalities of those who labored day after day to build and beautify this sacred space.

The high vaulting bosses of the north transept remain uncarved, one of numerous projects that await the creativity and resources of future stewards of the Cathedral.

The Parclose Stairway

At the northeast corner of the north transept, a stairway provides access from the nave to the crypt below. Known as the parclose stairway, this passage is defined by a fine example of pierced limestone tracery carved in situ by Italo Fanfani (1885–1943). The four small figures set in canopied niches in the upper portion of the screen honor churchmen and statesmen for their roles as cathedral builders: Edward the Confessor (d. 1066), King of England, who built Westminster Abbey; William of Wykeham (1324–1404), associated with Winchester Cathedral; Suger (d. 1151), Abbot of the Church of St. Denis, known as the father of Gothic architecture; and Louis IX (1214–1270), who built Sainte Chapelle, an outstanding Gothic chapel.

A bronze statue installed in the upper landing of the parclose stairway shows Abraham Lincoln kneeling in prayer. The sculptor, Herbert Spencer Houck (1876–1931), drew upon his own family lore for inspiration: Houck's father, a chaplain in the Union Army during the Civil War, had recounted for his children the experiences of standing near Lincoln at Gettysburg when the president delivered the famous Gettysburg Address and of walking in the woods near Gettysburg and coming upon Lincoln, alone and on his knees in prayer. While scholars have disputed the notion that Lincoln could have slipped away from crowds and dignitaries for such a solitary moment, the story became the basis for this enduring image.

THE NAVE

A procession of massive piers, called the main arcade, supports the triforium and clerestory levels of the majestic nave of the Cathedral and defines the main area used for congregational seating. North and south outer aisles beyond these piers run the entire length of the nave. In architectural terms, bays are the subdivisions into which the nave, as well as the chancel and transepts, are divided. Each bay consists of a pair of piers linked by a pointed arch, with triforium openings, a clerestory window, and a section of the vaulted ceiling above. In another sense, the bays mark the building units of the Cathedral, measuring the stages of construction, bay-by-bay, over eight decades and as funds became available. The Cathedral, then, consists of an eight-bay nave and five-bay chancel, intersected by a six-bay transept.

The Stained Glass

In the nave of the Cathedral there are three tiers of windows on the north and south sides: the windows of the outer aisles, the windows of the main arcade, and the clerestory.

The outer aisles, which flank the nave, were created by piercing the buttresses and enclosing the space between with masonry frames for the stained glass windows. In all, there are twenty-five outer aisle windows. A typical bay contains a pair of two-lancet windows, but some contain a single one-, two-, or three-lancet window. Unlike the windows of the clerestory, the subjects of the outer aisle windows, and the styles in which they are expressed, do not adhere to a single iconographic scheme, but rather embellish the themes of the individual bays in which they are placed, usually taking inspiration from some aspect of the life of the person for whom the bay is a memorial. Positioned near eye level, the windows are ideal for close examination of the craftsmanship involved in the art of stained glass.

The sixteen windows of the main arcade, above the roofline of the outer aisles, are a celebration of history, depicting outstanding men and women who have contributed to the Christian heritage. The windows of the north arcade depict Christian kings, spiritual and political leaders, and philosophers who worked through the framework of government and politics to express their faith and create

a more compassionate and civil world. Among them are Socrates, Plato, William Penn, Stephen Langton, John Marshall, Brother Lawrence, and Joan of Arc. In the south arcade, the windows commemorate people whose faith has informed a variety of aspirations and achievements in the professional arts. The themes of these windows include the healing arts, poets and writers, architects and sculptors, artisans and craftspeople, musicians and composers, and religious painters. In addition to such biblical figures as the prophet Elisha, King Solomon, and the prophetess and judge, Deborah, numerous historical figures are depicted, among them, Walter Reed, Marie Curie, John Milton, Dante Alighieri, Michelangelo Buonarroti, Sir Christopher Wren, Johann Sebastian Bach, and Rembrandt van Rijn.

One window on the south side stands out in striking contrast to the rest. Known as the *Space* window, this dramatic stained glass artwork was designed by Rodney Winfield (b. 1925) as a single scene spanning three lancets, instead

✣ *RODNEY WINFIELD'S SPACE WINDOW CONTAINS A SMALL SLIVER OF A MOON ROCK BROUGHT BACK TO EARTH BY THE APOLLO 11 ASTRONAUTS.*

Great windows, great music, great architecture, all
have a cosmic quality. . . they need no interpreter.
They are the voice of God in the soul of man.

—JAMES SHELDON,
Cathedral benefactor and stained glass scholar, 1938

of the more common grouping of three images, related but distinct, in each of three lancets. The colorful spheres suggest planets floating in the deep blue of space. The thin white line circling the spheres represents the trajectory of the spacecraft Apollo 11, reinforcing the sense that humanity is just a small part of the boundless universe. A small round piece of white glass in the center of a large red sphere contains a sliver of moon rock brought back from the first manned lunar landing in 1973 by the Apollo 11 astronauts, one of whom, Michael Collins, attended St. Albans School on the Cathedral Close. Several boss stones in the vaulting near the window continue the theme of space exploration. One depicts the surface of the moon, carved with craters and astronaut footprints.

The Memorial Bays
As the Cathedral grew from dream to reality, some of the founders expressed the hope that the Cathedral might become the "Westminster Abbey of America." However, architect Philip H. Frohman was aware that the accumulation of tombs, statues, and inscribed tablets had somewhat obscured the architecture of the abbey's interior. For Washington's cathedral, therefore, Frohman designated the bays in the outer aisles of the nave as areas where memorials could be placed without detracting from the harmony of the nave and transepts.

In all, there are sixteen memorial bays in the nave. The details of their decoration are not part of the formal iconographic scheme of the Cathedral. Rather, fifteen of the bays commemorate prominent Americans and Cathedral luminaries, the design of each chosen in consultation with the bay's donor, while the sixteenth bay honors the work of the National Cathedral Association (NCA). In this way, the bays also uphold a traditional use of the nave, which in medieval times was understood to be a place for secular use by the people,

often a place for meeting, commerce, and trade. The bays, moreover, capture specific moments in the history of the Cathedral's construction, each structural segment recording the time, place, and priorities of donors who aspired to build the Cathedral. The embellishments in each of these intimate spaces include symbolic and decorative elements related to the person for whom the bay is a memorial, often including references to their spiritual concerns, celebrated public achievements, and civic involvements, as well as more personal details.

One example is the first bay on the south side of the nave, which pays tribute to Andrew W. Mellon, who generously donated his art collection and substantial funds for the formation of the National Gallery of Art in Washington, D.C. A wrought iron gate lends a sense of privacy to this space, which is intended as an area for personal prayer and meditation. One of the noteworthy furnishings in the bay is a Coventry Cathedral Cross of Nails, which commemorates the English cathedral destroyed by bombing raids in 1940. The cross is fashioned from fourteenth-century nails once used to support the roof beams of Coventry Cathedral. Similar crosses have been distributed to persons and places on five continents. Consequently, the Coventry Cathedral Cross of Nails has become an international symbol of peace and reconciliation. The capitals of the four columns inside the bay are by sculptor Heinz Warneke. Three of the capitals symbolize earth, sea, and air, with more than thirty carved animals, birds, and fish worked into the designs. The façade of the National Gallery of Art appears on the capital of the fourth column, and a flowing vine, with a full-grown melon, provides a playful pun on the philanthropist's name. Moments in the history of the Presbyterian Church, of which Mellon was a member, are celebrated in a single-lancet window.

Other memorial bays on the south outer aisle include the Lee-Jackson Bay, which honors Confederate Generals Robert E. Lee and Thomas "Stonewall" Jackson; the Warren Bay,

which pays tribute to Charles Warren, a distinguished lawyer and historian of the Supreme Court; the Folger Bay, a gift of John Clifford and Kathrine Dulin Folger, which recalls the Lewis and Clark expedition and celebrates the natural beauty of America in the stained glass windows; and the Maryland Bay, also known as the Ellicott Memorial Bay, which was given in memory of three daughters of Maryland, Anna Campbell Ellicott and her sisters, Charlotte Campbell Nelson and Ella Campbell Smythe. Embellished with symbols of the state of Maryland, this bay also honors the historic role Maryland has played in the American Anglican church: the 1649 Maryland Toleration Act granted freedom of religious expression to all Christians; the first Bishop of Maryland, Thomas John Claggett, was also the first Episcopal bishop consecrated on American soil; and, until 1895, the Episcopal Diocese of Maryland encompassed the area now included in the Episcopal Diocese of Washington.

On the north outer aisle, memorial bays include the Dulin Bay, which honors Hanson Lee and Eugenia Bell Dulin and their support of the American Red Cross and Boys Clubs; the Bettelheim Bay, which is a memorial to Edwin Sumner Bettelheim, soldier and author; the White Bay, which, with its theme of peace and universal unity, memorializes the Honorable Henry White, a prominent United States diplomat during the 1890s and early 1900s and a signer of the Treaty of Versailles (ending World War I); the Boardman Bay, also known as the Humanitarian Bay, which pays tribute to Mabel Thorp Boardman, an American philanthropist and leader of the American Red Cross in the early twen-

tieth century; and the Kellogg Bay, which, with its theme of universal peace, honors Frank Billings Kellogg, senator, ambassador, secretary of state, and Nobel Peace laureate, whose multilateral Kellogg-Briand Pact of 1928 prohibited war as an instrument of national policy.

One of several bays that record milestones in the history of the Cathedral is the Glover Bay, the fifth bay on the south outer aisle. Also known as Founders' Bay, it honors Charles Carroll Glover and his wife, Annie Cunningham Glover, whose home was the site of an important meeting, on December 8, 1891, to promote the idea of the Cathedral. The windows in the bay explore the theme of humanity's search for God. In these lancets, which feature transparent glass mixed with large, hand-blown slabs of vibrant ruby red, the artists Rowan and Irene Matz LeCompte (1926–1970) worked with an array of secular and religious images. The eastern lancet portrays the prophet Jeremiah shackled in chains, symbolic of his imprisonment. Pictured beneath him is the city of Washington. In the upper portion, the prophet is shown holding an evergreen tree,

symbol of continuity and everlasting life. In the adjoining lancet, St. Paul is seen as he preached on Mars Hill, or Areopagus, in Athens. In the western lancets, Jacob is shown on the left, building an altar to the Lord. His altar is built of "stones" that are symbolic representations of human life and labor in the New World: a wigwam, an immigrant ship, a colonial meeting house, and a mill. In the lower portion of the right lancet, the artists have included a small group of people sitting in conversation, an allusion to the historic meeting to discuss the possibility of building the Cathedral. Nearby is an image of the Glover home on Lafayette Square near the White House, where that meeting took place.

While the Founders' Bay memorializes a pivotal moment in the inception of the Cathedral, the National Cathedral Association Bay, the fourth bay on the north side of the nave, honors the decades-long dedication of NCA members. Since its formation in 1899, before the Cathedral's Foundation Stone had been laid, the NCA has steadfastly supported all aspects of the Cathedral's construction, maintenance, and ministry. The group has provided funds not only for the construction of this bay, but also for the Women's Porch on the north transept, the west narthex marble floor, the Pilgrim Observation Gallery, the Perry Auditorium, and the NCA pinnacle on the south tower. The NCA Bay was dedicated in 1963 and contains a pair of two-lancet windows designed and executed by Hungarian artist Ervin Bossanyi (1891–1975) that depict the role of the Christian woman as lifegiver, healer, purifier, and teacher.

Another bay that commemorates a major facet of the history of the Cathedral is the Frohman Bay, on the north outer aisle. Philip H. Frohman was architect of Washington National Cathedral for fifty years, from 1921 to 1971. He refined the original architectural plans by Bodley and Vaugh-

an into the structure that is the national treasure we know today. Frohman, who once said that Gothic architecture was the driving force of his life, visited Bethlehem Chapel in 1914, which at the time was the only completed portion of the Cathedral. In the guest register, the twenty-seven-year-old Frohman wrote, in a coded message, a prayer that he might one day become the architect of this great cathedral. Seven years later, he did.

The Book of Remembrance
A large carved-oak case, located in the Kellogg Bay, contains the Cathedral's Book of Remembrance. Since 1898, every gift given in memory of, thanksgiving for, or in honor of individuals or events has been recorded in the Book of Remem-

✢ AT SOME POINT EACH DAY, LEE LAWRIE'S STATUE OF GEORGE WASHINGTON IS AWASH IN THE COLORS FROM ROBERT PINART'S "FOUNDING OF A NEW NATION" WINDOW IN THE WASHINGTON BAY.

brance. There are almost one hundred volumes to date and each year approximately 2,700 names are added. The case also houses books listing the names of those who have contributed needlepoint for the Cathedral and volunteer members of All Hallows Guild, stewards of the Cathedral grounds.

PRESIDENTIAL MEMORIALS

In its role as a church for the nation, the Cathedral has incorporated into its decorative scheme several memorials to past presidents of the United States. The two bays flanking the main doors of the west nave are dedicated to George Washington, on the south side, and Abraham Lincoln, on the north side. The tomb of President Woodrow Wilson, the only president buried in the District of Columbia, resides on the south side in the third bay, which bears his name.

Washington Bay

The heroic statue of George Washington was the work of sculptor Lee Lawrie (1877–1963), who said, "I have tried to show not the soldier, not the President, but the man Washington, coming into Christ Church, Alexandria, pausing a moment before going down the aisle to his pew."

The Washington figure, one of the few large freestanding sculptures in the Cathedral, is seven feet, six inches tall and is carved of pure white Vermont marble. The many facets of Washington's long career are reflected in the words carved on each side of the base of the pedestal: First Citizen, Churchman, President, Statesman, Farmer, Soldier, Patriot, and Freemason.

The surrounding alcove is filled with carvings symbolic of Washington's life and achievements. The carving on the tympanum over the doorway emphasizes Washington's life as both farmer and soldier. The center of this stone is dominated by the Washington family coat of arms, which was later adopted by the District of Columbia for its flag. On the left is the figure of a farmer with a tobacco leaf in one hand; on the right is a figure outfitted in the uniform of a Continental Army officer. The entire tympanum is encircled with a border of holly leaves, an allusion to the holly trees at Washington's beloved home, Mount Vernon.

Label mould terminations on each side of the doorway include carvings of the façades of Mount Vernon and Independence Hall in Philadelphia. The seals of the Commonwealth of Virginia and the Armed Forces Institute of Heraldry are carved in these stones in low relief.

The abstract stained glass window, designed by Robert Pinart, celebrates the founding of the new nation. Each color evokes an aspect of the search for freedom, with the dark colors representing tyranny and the reds signifying the blood lost in America's revolutionary struggle. Another smaller window, above the entrance to the outer aisle, by artist Brenda Belfield (b. 1938) honors George Washington's devoted wife, Martha.

In the floor of the bay is a seal representing the thirteen original states of the young nation Washington governed.

Lincoln Bay

The Lincoln Bay, the first bay at the west end of the nave's north aisle, is dedicated to the memory of President Abra-

ham Lincoln. The heroic bronze statue by sculptor Walker K. Hancock shows Lincoln as he was leaving his home in Springfield, Illinois, to come to Washington and assume the presidency. The words inscribed on the wall next to the statue are taken from his farewell speech to the people of Springfield, delivered as he stood on the rear platform of the train.

Carved in the tympanum over the north door, a pair of hands clasping an olive branch symbolizes Lincoln's effort to unite North and South during the Civil War, while the bosses overhead illustrate stanzas from the *Battle Hymn of the Republic*. The carvings on the label mould terminations depict the caps of the infantrymen of the Union and Confederate armies. Lighting the Lincoln Bay and positioned vertically between the outer aisle and main arcade is a three-lancet window, an abstract design by Robert Pinart, that symbolizes the agony of civil war. The deep reds and purples suggest the blood of the battlefield and the assassination of President Lincoln. The blues and grays represent the Union and Confederate states, while the golds and yellows suggest fields of wheat and corn that signal a return to peace. Carved in the stone beneath the window are the names of Robert Todd Lincoln, Mary Lincoln Isham, and Lincoln Isham, Lincoln descendents and Cathedral benefactors. Robert Todd Lincoln, the president's only surviving son, left a sum of money to his daughter, Mary, who, in turn, left the money to her son, Lincoln, who donated the funds for the inclusion of the Lincoln Bay in the Cathedral. Nearby is a single lancet window by Brenda Belfield that memorializes the women who raised Lincoln: his mother, Nancy Hanks Lincoln, and his stepmother, Sarah Bush Lincoln.

The central panel in the marble floor of this bay contains a five-pointed star composed of twenty-one Lincoln-head pennies set in a circle of buff-colored terrazzo. It is surrounded by a green marble ring delineated by copper strips and containing thirteen pennies. The thirty-four coins symbolize the number of states in the Union at the time of Lincoln's inauguration in 1861. The central coin is placed face down to indicate South Carolina's secession from the Union two months before the beginning of Lincoln's administration.

"You are here to enrich the world. You impoverish yourself if you forget this errand."
—Woodrow Wilson

Wilson Bay

Following his death in 1924, President Woodrow Wilson was buried in Bethlehem Chapel in the crypt of the Cathedral. The tomb was moved to the memorial bay that bears his name in 1956, the centenary of Wilson's birth. The presence of Wilson's tomb in the Cathedral has a personal dimension: Wilson's grandson, Francis B. Sayre, Jr., served as dean of the Cathedral from 1951 to 1978. In fact, Dean Sayre's earliest memory of the Cathedral was as a child, riding in a Pierce-Arrow automobile up Embassy Row on Massachusetts Avenue to Mount St. Alban with his grandfather, President Wilson, beside him.

The tomb and the surrounding bay are embellished with remembrances of the life and achievements of the president. On the tomb itself rests the crusader's sword, in memory of Wilson's valiant battle for world peace following World War I. Thistles at the terminations of the cross-shaped hilt allude to his Scottish heritage. On the side of the sarcophagus facing the nave are the seals of the places where Wilson provided inspired leadership: Princeton University, the State of New Jersey, and the United States.

The thematic unity of the bay is reinforced by quotations, inscribed on each wall, from Wilson's speeches: his first Inaugural Address; his war message to the U. S. Congress; his speech submitting the Treaty of Versailles to the Senate; and his last published words, in which he professed the Christian faith that had served as the root of his phi-

losophy. The north vaulting boss depicts ivy leaves and the coats-of-arms of the World War I allies: the United States, England, France, Italy, and Belgium. The south vaulting boss is carved with images of World War I personnel: an army officer, a private, a nurse, and a non-commissioned naval officer.

Among the finest works by Ervin Bossanyi, the windows in the Wilson Bay depict war and peace through the lens of Christian faith. The left lancet represents peace as God gives it, blessing his children. The middle lancet represents God's forgiveness for humankind through the sacrifice of Christ. The third lancet depicts peace as humankind destroys it.

The corbels on the two niche sculptures in the Wilson Bay depict the Staunton, Virginia, home where President Wilson was born, and Nassau Hall at Princeton University, where Wilson served as president from 1902 to 1910.

ANOMALIES OF ARCHITECTURE

From the outset, one of the guiding principles at Washington National Cathedral has been the pursuit of perfection in craftsmanship. Imperfections, however, have found their way, intentionally and otherwise, into the structure of the Cathedral, providing opportunities for humor, humility, and, paradoxically, greater beauty. In War Memorial Chapel, an error in calculations produced a capital stone that was a fraction of an inch too short. When Cathedral architect Philip Frohman discovered his error, he set about correcting it. At his own expense, he commissioned two carved figures and inserted them to conceal the space. These carvings, known as "The Architect's Mistake," depict two images of the architect: tearing his hair out at the realization of the mistake and then, in an

"aha" moment, discovering a solution.

In the nave, there is a discrepancy in size from one pier to another. Furthermore, the east-west axis of the building is askew. The apse itself is not on a true east-west axis. At the crossing, an intentional shift in the axis occurs and the nave is shifted, with the result that the figure of Adam in the center west portal is six feet north of the projected center line of the choir. This break in axis is aesthetically motivated and achieves Frohman's intent to give the best visual perspective from the west portals and prevent the perception of the converging of lines that a continuous, straight axis would have produced. Often, an ecclesiastical theory for this shift refers to the floor plan of the building as a symbol of Christ's broken body on the Cross, with his head askew. An alternative explanation proffered for this and other "intentional flaws" involves the medieval precedent of deliberate asymmetries that acknowledge in their imperfection that only God can be perfect.

Cathedrals do not belong to a single generation. They are churches of history. They gather up the faith of a whole people. . . as they have hoped and suffered and believed, across the centuries.

— DEAN FRANCIS B. SAYRE, JR.

ARCHITECTURAL AND DECORATIVE CARVINGS IN THE NAVE

The Cathedral architects incorporated many niches in the walls of this Gothic structure as a means of enhancing the building's otherwise austere architecture. The niches, with their sculptured figures, add visual interest, create rich patterns of light and shadow, and relieve the visual weight of the massive stone structure.

Mindful of Dean Sayre's ecumenical efforts to have a cathedral that would acknowledge all branches of Christendom, the architect decided on a series of "Saints of All Nations" for the niche figures in the outer aisles of the nave. In the early Church, all members were called saints; later, all members were called Christians. In keeping with that early Christian spirit of inclusion, the individuals represented in the series of niche figures did not have to be canonized or otherwise recognized by Church authorities to qualify as saints. In the Wilson Bay, for example, the two niche figures are of St. Andrew (Scotland) and John Calvin (France and Switzerland). In the NCA Bay, the niche statues represent St. Theresa of Avila (Spain) and Isabella Thoburn, a Methodist missionary to India. In Glover Bay, there are statues of St. Gregory (Armenia) and John Hus, a fifteenth-century reformer (Bohemia). And in Mellon Bay, the two niche statues portray Joan of Arc (France) and St. Patrick (Ireland). Other figures include Toyohiko Kagawa (Japan), Desiderius Erasmus (Holland), Martin Luther (Germany), and Ulrich Zwingli (Switzerland).

In the south aisle of the nave, the vaulting corbels are adorned with traditional foliage and a variety of symbols. Those in the north aisle portray great modern Christians, "modern" meaning that an actual photographic image of each subject was

✣ *THE STATUARY IN THE NORTH AISLE DEPICTS THOSE, SUCH AS ALBERT SCHWEITZER, WHO PRAISE GOD THROUGH THEIR GOOD WORKS.*

available. These corbel sculptures support one of the nave's iconographic themes, the role of the faithful in the Christian era. Among the figures portrayed are Dietrich Bonhoeffer, Jane Addams, Helen Keller, Pope John XXIII, and Martin Luther King, Jr. With the exception of the depiction of Albert Schweitzer, which was carved by Roger Morigi, Cathedral artist Constantine Seferlis (1930–2005) carved all of these sculptures.

After the vaulting bosses, stones called label mould terminations comprise the largest series of carvings in the Cathedral. Their subject matter varies: some are carved with a sacred or commemorative theme and others are more purely decorative.

✣ *CARVER CONSTANTINE SEFERLIS CARVED THE STATUES IN THE NORTH AND SOUTH AISLES, INCLUDING THAT OF JOAN OF ARC IN THE MELLON BAY.*

Among the finest iconographic termination stones are those in the main arcade of the nave, where the piers intersect with the arches they support. These, along with the boss stones at the apex of each arch, form triads, each of which depicts a biblical story of human encounter with the divine. Those on the north side present stories from the Hebrew scriptures, among these the sacrifice of Isaac, Moses and the burning bush, Hagar giving Ishmael water, and David with a sling in his hand. Those on the south side recount stories from the Book of Acts, such as Cornelius praying, Peter in a trance, the death of Stephen, as well as Pentecost, and the Ascension.

OTHER POINTS OF INTEREST

Besides serving as the transition from the secular to the spiritual world, the narthex is the connecting point between two spaces representative of the Cathedral's dedication to the political, cultural, and economic rights of every human being. On the north side is the Human Rights Porch and on the south, the Churchill Porch, both evoking a history of heroic support of the rights of others. From here, also, visitors can make their way to an oak-paneled exhibit and reception area. On the north and south sides of the narthex are elevators leading to the Pilgrim Observation Gallery, with its dramatic views of Maryland and Virginia, and the Perry Auditorium, where Cathedral-related programs and meetings are held.

The Human Rights Porch

On the north side of the narthex, at the base of St. Peter Tower, is the Human Rights Porch, a space reserved for tributes to those who have made extraordinary contributions to the advancement of human equality. Among the many examples of embellishments still to be completed in the Cathedral fabric are the label mould terminations in this porch, which remain uncarved. For the present, they may be seen as reminders of the unfinished work of reconciliation facing the human family.

Three niche figures in the passage to the north-west cloister honor champions of human rights: Archbishop Oscar Romero (1917–1980), Bishop John Walker (1925–1989), and First Lady Eleanor Roosevelt (1884–1962). One of the most recent additions to the stone carvings in the Cathedral is a half-boss located in the low vaulting of this intimate space. Its design is an interpretation of the passage from the Book of the

Prophet Amos, "Let justice roll down like waters and righteousness like an ever flowing stream." The carving, unusual for its concave, rather than convex, shape, features water cascading into a pool and then transforming, as it moves counterclockwise, into the figures of a man, woman, and child on the bank as they are being freed from the bonds of injustice and oppression. From the man's wrist hangs a broken chain symbolizing the triumph of freedom.

❖ *SCULPTURES IN THE HUMAN RIGHTS PORCH HONOR CHAMPIONS OF HUMAN RIGHTS, SUCH AS THE EL SALVADORIAN MARTYR, ARCHBISHOP OSCAR ROMERO, AND AMERICA'S FIRST LADY AND GOOD WILL AMBASSADOR, ELEANOR ROOSEVELT.*

The abstract leaf-like imagery of the three-lancet window lighting the Human Rights Porch refers to God's healing through natural herbs and medicines. The darker background colors signify the pain and mystery of illness; the lighter colors, especially in the center lancet, signify the hope and healing that are gifts from God's natural world.

The Churchill Porch

On the south side of the narthex, the base of the St. Paul Tower forms an interior porch dedicated to Sir Winston Churchill (1874–1965) in recognition of his contributions to humanity's fight against tyranny during World War II. The niche statues in the adjacent vestibule depict three prominent men in the development of English common law: Stephen

Langton (1150–1228), Simon de Montfort (1208–1265), and Sir Edward Coke (1552–1634). At the peak of the vaulting, forty-nine feet above the floor, is a large limestone boss carved with the coats-of-arms of Great Britain and of the United States, signifying Churchill's dual citizenship.

In the south gallery of the porch, a three-lancet abstract window alludes to Churchill's worldwide radio address on April 27, 1941, in which, quoting a poem by Arthur Hugh Clough, Churchill expressed his hopes for assistance from America as Great Britain stood alone fighting the Axis Powers. English artist John Piper (1903–1992) took

✣ *One of the Cathedral's most cherished treasures— a first edition of the King James Bible*

as inspiration for his design that broadcast and, specifically, these lines from Clough's poem:

> *And not by eastern windows only,*
> *When daylight comes, comes in the light;*
> *In front the sun climbs slow, how slowly!*
> *But westward, look, the land is bright!*

The Rare Book Library

The Rare Book Library, opened in 1965, occupies the southwest wing flanking the base of the St. Paul Tower. The upper level provides space for exhibitions, receptions, and other gatherings. The library's principal exhibit room is paneled in oak, with oak pilasters and beams. The focal point of the room is a limestone exhibit case, carved with delicate crockets, finials, and small faces. It was designed to house the library's treasure, a first edition of the King James Bible. Printed in London by Robert Barker in 1611, it is the "Prince Henry" copy, meaning it belonged to Henry, Prince of Wales, the eldest son of the King after whom the authorized version is named. The book is bound in dark red morocco and bears the prince's arms. One level below the exhibit room, and in an area closed to the public, the library space serves as a repository for an important collection of Bibles and Books of Common Prayer in English and many other languages.

The Pilgrim Observation Gallery and Perry Auditorium

Accessed by elevators located in the narthex, the Pilgrim Observation Gallery occupies the seventh floor of the west towers. From this Gallery, the highest point in Washington accessible to the public, visitors are welcomed to view the beautiful city, its monuments, parks, and landmarks. On a cloudless day this dramatic, nearly 360-degree panorama includes Maryland, Virginia, and even the distant peaks of the Blue Ridge Mountains. From the gallery's seventy windows, the great and small marvels of the Cathedral's Gothic architecture are also visible: the Gloria in Excelsis tower, flying buttresses, carved pinnacles, gargoyles and grotesques, and cherubim and seraphim.

On the same level as the observation gallery and situated over the nave, is Perry Auditorium, named for the Rev. Canon Charles Perry, Cathedral Provost during the final years of construction. The auditorium, which is used for lectures, meetings, and programs, seats almost two hundred people. ■

The Lower Level

THE LOWER LEVEL, OR CRYPT, of Washington National Cathedral contains four chapels, as well as burial vaults, storerooms, and workrooms located along two parallel corridors running the length of the building on both the north and south side. Three of the crypt chapels mark key moments in the life of Jesus Christ, underscoring His humanity as well as His divinity. Bethlehem Chapel celebrates His humble birth, the Chapel of St. Joseph of Arimathea recalls His earthly death, and the Chapel of the Resurrection, His triumph over death. Proclaiming a theology of the incarnate God, these chapels serve as a figurative, as well as a literal, foundation for the soaring edifice above them. A fourth chapel, an alcove just off the passageway leading to the Garth, is the tiny Chapel of the Good Shepherd, which represents the loving, caring God and provides a place of solace and prayer for individuals in times of crisis or need.

The North and South Crypt Aisles

Two aisles span the length of the Cathedral crypt, providing access to the chapels and other areas. Only the south aisle is fully accessible to the public, stretching from "The Way of Peace" entrance, in the east, through the Museum Store, which supports the Cathedral through sales of religious gift items, books, and recorded music, to a stairwell at the west end that leads to the narthex. A portion of the north aisle services offices, storage areas, and classrooms. These two aisles, with their rounded arches, thick columns, low ceilings, and feeling of massive weight, recall the Norman Romanesque style of architecture that preceded the Gothic. This arrange-

HILDRETH MEIERE'S STUNNING MOSAIC OF THE RESURRECTED CHRIST, IN THE CHAPEL OF THE RESURRECTION

✤ *An alabaster angel in prayerful watch over the tomb of Bishop Henry Yates Satterlee in Bethlehem Chapel*

ment echoes Old World architectural ancestors of the Cathedral. Many Gothic churches were built upon the foundations of structures built in an earlier style.

The oldest entrance into the Cathedral, at the southeast corner, is called "The Way of Peace." These words from the song of Zacharias appear in relief on the exterior lintel of the door. Above the inner vestibule doors is a niche bearing a statue of the Reverend Robert Hunt (d.1608), the first priest of the Church of England resident in Virginia and vicar of the Jamestown colony for two years. Mounted in the wall under the statue is a brick from Rev. Hunt's Jamestown church.

Opposite the door to Bethlehem Chapel, in the south wall of the aisle, is the tomb of Frederick H. Prince and his wife, Abigail, early Cathedral benefactors and parents of the young aviator memorialized in St. John's Chapel on the nave level of the Cathedral.

The south crypt aisle houses fine examples of wrought iron grillwork by Samuel Yellin. His work is concentrated in the east end of the Cathedral, in the crypt and nave, because these portions of the building were completed at the height of his career and before his death in 1940. The large gates at the easternmost end of the south aisle, known as the Jennings

LIVING STONES

Over the decades, sacred and secular stones have been given to and embedded into the framework of the Cathedral, making manifest a spirituality of relationship. This deeply rooted tradition can be traced to the Cathedral's Foundation Stone, laid in 1907. Set into the block of American granite is a smaller stone from the field adjoining the Church of the Holy Nativity in Bethlehem.

In 1920, the Cathedral received a block of reddish-hued granite from Mt. Sinai. The block was cut into ten smaller blocks and set in the footpace of marble before the High Altar as a physical reminder of the Ten Commandments. The High Altar itself is constructed of twelve stones from Solomon's quarry just outside Jerusalem.

Secular connections are similarly recorded. In the wall of the North Cloister stairs is a stone engraved with the word "GITMO," an abbrevi-

ation for Guantanamo Bay. The stone, with its simple inscription, was given to the Cathedral by the officers and men of Guantanamo Bay Naval Base, in appreciation for a 1964 visit made by Dean Francis Sayre. In the War Memorial Chapel, marked by neither plaque nor inscription, is a stone given by the White House during the residence's renovation in the 1950s.

Elsewhere, stones from the Appian Way, the Western Wall in Jerusalem, Westminster Abbey, Glastonbury Abbey, Canterbury Cathedral, numerous other

ORNAMENTED FIRST CENTURY STONE FRAGMENT FROM ALONG THE APPIAN WAY (QUEEN OF ROADS) LEADING INTO ROME

cathedrals in England, Wales, and France, and even the moon have been worked into the Cathedral, its furnishings, and its grounds.

The gesture of incorporating sacred and secular stones into the Cathedral has, on at least one occasion, been reversed. In 1957, Dean Sayre gave a Cathedral stone to the newly constructed Temple Sinai. The Reform Jewish congregation had, for five years, made Washington National Cathedral its semi-permanent home, worshipping every Friday night in Bethlehem Chapel during the construction of its synagogue. On the last of the Friday services in the Cathedral chapel, Dean Sayre presented the stone, which was later placed in the temple's sanctuary wall as a token of the shared ground upon which our mutual faith traditions are built.

This grafting of old and new, sacred and secular, Christian and non-Christian expresses the sense of continuity with the past and the sense of interconnection that inform the Christian faith and the identity of the Cathedral.

reads: "I am the vine, ye are the branches thereof." Installed in 1952, these gates were commissioned in memory of Anne Ray Godart.

The crypt aisles are richly arrayed with such reminders of the past—memorials to men and women, prominent and obscure, who have preceded us. The walls of both aisles are intermittently adorned with memorial tablets, some honoring those interred elsewhere in the Cathedral. In the south aisle, a tablet memorializes Admiral Gaspard de Coligny, one of the martyrs in the Saint Bartholomew massacre in Paris in 1572. Another, presented by the District of Columbia chapter of the Daughters of 1812, pays tribute to Frances Scott Key (1780–1845), author of *The Star Spangled Banner*. Another recalls the life of Archibald Willingham Butt (1865–1912), a military aide to President Theodore Roosevelt who perished aboard the *Titanic*. Others memorialize those who served the Episcopal Diocese of Washington and the Cathedral. Among these are Edgar Priest, first organist and choirmaster of the Cathedral, and Bishop John Claggett, first Episcopal Bishop of Maryland. Finally, the cross-aisle columbarium serves as the place of interment for deans of the Cathedral, bishops of the Episcopal Diocese of Washington, and their spouses. William F. Creighton (1909–1987), fifth Bishop of Washington, was the first bishop to be interred in this columbarium. Beside him is Bishop John Thomas Walker (1925–1989), sixth Bishop of Washington and Cathedral dean.

Just through the cross-aisle columbarium and above its northern arch is a niche containing a statue of St. Margaret of Scotland, dedicated in 1967 in memory of Helene Alexander Johnson, who had been a volunteer docent at the Cathedral. St. Margaret, canonized in 1250, was known for her personal piety demonstrated through a life of prayer and generosity. (A niche on the south aisle in parallel position remains empty.) A few steps above this aisle and on the east

Memorial Gates, were installed in 1933. The cresting bar atop these gates contains a cross with stylized irises, which symbolize the Resurrection, springing from each arm. The unusual height of the bar allows a crucifer to process through the gates during a service without needing to lower his or her cross.

To the left, after passing through the Jennings Gates, another Yellin work, the 1931 Janney Gate, closes off the entrance to the chamber holding the burial board on which are inscribed the names of all who are interred in the Cathedral. The gate is topped with spears, symbolizing protection of the dead, an image that originated from medieval knights casting their spears into the ground to protect their fallen leader.

Iron gates at each end of the cross-aisle columbarium connecting the north and south aisles were wrought by Theodore Voss (1901–1975) and bear images of grape vines whose branches, leaves, and clusters of grapes are intertwined in an intricate design. An inscription at the top of each gate

"In years to come wherever you may go in Washington or its environs you will catch a sudden glimpse of the Cathedral rising on Mount Saint Alban and you will know it to be, truly, a witness for Christ in the heart of America."

—BISHOP HENRY YATES SATTERLEE, *1898*

side of a landing of the parclose stairway, is tucked a diminutive window that presents an image of Jesus as the good shepherd with one of David, the most famous shepherd of the Hebrew Testament. David is shown soothing his sheep with the strumming of his harp and song. The words of the Twenty-third Psalm are crafted into the window and a musical staff conveys the musical talent for which David was known.

✥ ESTABLISHED IN THE 1950S BY DEAN FRANCIS SAYRE, JR., GOOD SHEPHERD CHAPEL IS FOR THOSE WHO SEEK COMFORT AND SUCCOR OR SIMPLY A QUIET MOMENT OF SELF-REFLECTION.

The portion of the north aisle accessible to visitors provides access to Bethlehem Chapel in the east and extends westward to the north entrance of the Chapel of St. Joseph of Arimathea. Like the eastern portion of the south aisle, the north aisle is lit by a series of stained glass windows that are among the first installed in the Cathedral. A short passage provides access to the Chapel of the Good Shepherd and connects the north crypt aisle to the outdoors via the Garth Cloister. Among the most recent architectural features to be installed in the Cathedral is a gate placed in this passage near the Chapel of the Good Shepherd. This gate was designed and fabricated by renowned artist Albert Paley (b. 1944) of Rochester, New York. Paley's gate and grille provide a contemporary interpretation of two biblical passages: the first, the Twenty-third Psalm: "The Lord is my shepherd, I shall not want. He makes me lie down in green pastures; He leads me beside still waters. He restores my soul"; and the second, from the

Gospel of John: "I am the gate for the sheep. I came that they may have life and have it abundantly." The nine-foot-high steel gate teems with imagery inspired by these texts: A shepherd's crook, reeds, and other vegetation, still waters, and a gold-plated nimbus, whose interwoven rays and radiating circles extend across the gate. With the installation of the Paley work, the Cathedral affirms its continuing commitment to commission and install contemporary works of art that proclaim the Word.

The Chapel of the Good Shepherd

The Chapel of the Good Shepherd, located between the Paley Gate and the Garth Cloister, originally served as a receiving room for flower deliveries, but during Dean Sayre's tenure it was converted to a place for private prayer, in accordance with the role of the Cathedral as a sanctuary. It is open to worshippers from early morning until late evening each day and accessible from the Garth when the Cathedral is closed.

The reredos figure of Christ the shepherd tenderly carrying a lamb is the work of sculptor Walker Hancock and was carved by Roger Morigi in 1976. The Salisbury pink granite of the carving has acquired a patina almost the color of living flesh, owing to the many worshippers who, over time, have touched it. The carved wooden screen and pews were fabricated at St. Sidwell's Art Works, England. The modernist colorless glass windows in the chapel, the work of Robert Pinart, are designed to maximize the available sunlight in this deeply shaded corner of the building.

Bethlehem Chapel

The first portion of the Cathedral to be completed was Bethlehem Chapel, a memorial to Henry Yates Satterlee, the first Episcopal Bishop of Washington. Services have been held here every day since the chapel was opened in 1912. The altar

of Bethlehem Chapel is situated directly beneath the High Altar in the sanctuary overhead and rests above the Foundation Stone of the Cathedral below.

Bethlehem Chapel reflects a late-nineteenth- and early-twentieth-century perception of the Gothic architecture style. This Romantic and rather academic conception endeavored to replicate the fourteenth-century decorated Gothic style with such fastidiousness that the Neo-Gothic style effectively surpassed the reality of its historic models. Washington National Cathedral, in its infancy, was undoubtedly putting its best Gothic foot forward with this, its first chapel.

✣ *John Lisle's Pre-Raphaelite-influenced stained glass windows are among the most beautiful in the Cathedral.*

The center panel of the limestone altar reredos depicts the birth of Jesus, and was carved from a single block of stone. On the left and right of the bas-relief panel are the images of the four

evangelists, Matthew, Mark, Luke, and John, each with his emblem: the human, the lion, the ox, and the eagle.

In the ambulatory behind the altar is the tomb of Henry Yates Satterlee, the Cathedral's founding bishop. Carved of Welsh alabaster by the Nathaniel Hitch Company of London, England, the recumbent figure of the bishop is positioned so that its head is directly behind the center of the altar, which, in turn, is above the Foundation Stone, some distance below. The Foundation Stone is a single block of American granite embedded with a stone gathered from the fields near Bethlehem and etched with the words, "The Word was made flesh and dwelt among us." The stone was set in place at a service of dedication on the feast of St. Michael and All Angels, September 29, 1907.

The five windows in the ambulatory tell the Nativity story with colorful detail. Read from left to right, they do not, however, observe a strict chronology: *Genealogy, Gloria in Excelsis, Annunciation, Epiphany*, and *Nunc Dimittis* (the Canticle of Simeon). The central, if unusual, placement of the *Annunciation* window is a subtle tribute to Bishop Satterlee, who was ordained a priest and subsequently consecrated bishop on the feast of the Annunciation. John W. Lisle of Kempe and Company, London, designed the windows in the fifteenth-century English style, though strongly influenced by the Pre-Raphaelite movement of the mid- to late nineteenth century.

Admiral George Dewey, hero of the Spanish-American War and prominent supporter of the Cathedral, is also interred in Bethlehem Chapel. In 1898, as Bishop Satterlee contemplated signing the contract for the purchase of the Cathedral land, which would entail a substantial mortgage of $145,000, he approached his predicament with thoughts of Admiral Dewey at Manila: "...and how for the sake of his country he had taken his life in his hands; how, if he had been beaten at Manila, there was absolutely nowhere for his fleet to go; how they would be portless, coal less, homeless, disabled. Then I felt, 'If Dewey can do this for country, surely I can take a different kind of risk for God.'" The bishop signed the contract in the fall of 1898, and in 1899, Admiral Dewey became a member of the Cathedral Chapter.

The iconographic scheme of Bethlehem Chapel extends to the needlepoint kneelers, which bear symbols and images related to the Nativity story, including stars, mangers, camels, magi, shepherds, and angels. Designed and produced over a period of years by a variety of artists, the kneelers reflect

A Stitch in Time

At Washington National Cathedral, we employ both preservation and conservation methods in caring for the architecture and fabric of this magnificent place. Preservation techniques work to maintain an object or section of the building in its original condition, preventing deterioration and keeping all original elements intact. Conservation technologies, on the other hand, allow for sympathetic alteration when original materials have failed. A perfect example of the latter can be found in our needlepoint conservation work.

The Cathedral contains over 1,500 pieces of needlepoint, dating from 1954 to the present. After several decades, our well-used kneelers may begin to show their age. Stuffing often breaks down, either hardening into an uncomfortable lump or disintegrating into sand. Surfaces become grimy, canvases become weak, and sometimes the stitches simply wear out from years of use. If the actual needlepoint surface shows rips or slits, it may need to be refabricated, but complete replacement is less desirable than

preservation of existing needlepoint. Whenever possible, the original needlepoint is saved. The cushion's backing and stuffing are removed, the needlepoint surface is carefully cleaned, and the piece is re-blocked and/or inset into a velvet border to prolong use. As our oldest cushions pass the half-century mark, refabrication is becoming a necessity. The new pieces use the same design as the originals, but in most cases they are stitched on a more robust canvas with modern, longer-lasting stuffing. The originals are then unstuffed, cleaned, and stored flat in our needlepoint archive to serve as an important record for future generations of needlepoint stitchers.

many different styles, all unified, however, by the consistent deep red background color. The wall niches also contain statues of persons related to the Nativity and the lineage of Jesus: King David with his harp and Ruth with a sheaf of wheat on the south wall, and John the Baptizer and Anna the prophetess on the north wall.

The Chapel of St. Joseph of Arimathea

Directly beneath the great crossing, where the nave and transepts meet, is the chapel dedicated to St. Joseph of Arimathea, who gave his sepulcher as a tomb for the crucified Jesus. This chapel, with ironclad wooden doors and iron gates at the entrances, is twelve steps below the level of the rest of the crypt, symbolic of the descent into a tomb. In keeping with the medieval practice of building a Gothic cathedral over the crypt of an earlier church, the chapel reflects the Norman Romanesque style, the architecture that preceded the Gothic. Eight piers are evident in this chapel. Four relatively small pilasters define the shape of the chapel space, giving it the configuration of a Greek cross, while the group of four larger piers, each twenty-seven feet in diameter, support the central tower. Only one-quarter of each of the larg-

⁜ ABOVE: *A CONTEMPO-
RARY FOLK EUCHARIST IS
HELD IN THE CHAPEL OF
ST. JOSEPH OF ARIMATHEA
EACH SUNDAY, A TWENTY-
FIRST CENTURY CELEBRA-
TION AMID THE MASSIVE
NORMAN PIERS.*

⁜ LEFT: *JAN DE ROSEN'S
TEMPERA ON GOLD LEAF
MURAL PROVIDES A STUN-
NING FOCAL POINT IN
THE UNADORNED WORSHIP
SPACE OF THE CHAPEL.*

choirboys and Cathedral staff as models for his mural: the faces of St. Joseph of Arimathea and Jesus belong, respectively, to a Cathedral verger and a boiler man.

In the rear of the chapel, a wrought iron gate by Nol Putnam (b. 1934) guards the entrance to the Cathedral columbarium, which consists of three chambers lined with burial vaults. It is the final resting place of dozens of donors, artists, musicians, and others so honored for their dedication to the life of the Cathedral. The tympanum above the entrance to the columbarium is a deep bas-relief of a sleeping Roman soldier, the resurrected Christ holding a cross, and three women, Mary, the mother of Jesus, Mary Magdeline, and Mary Salome outside the empty tomb. On the southwest wall, a bronze plaque with an inscription in Braille honors an avid supporter and activist for the deaf and blind, author and lecturer Helen Keller (1880–1968). Keller is interred in the columbarium with Anne Sullivan Macy (1866–1936), her lifelong tutor and friend, and Keller's cherished companion, Mary Agnes "Polly" Thomson (1885–1960).

er piers is visible. The massive pillars of solid masonry and the rounded arches typify Norman construction, while the pointed arches over the altar and passage to the columbarium signal the transition to the Gothic style.

The centerpiece of the chapel is the painting above the altar, the only mural in the Cathedral. The scene depicts the entombment of Jesus, following his crucifixion. The three crosses on Calvary stand in the upper left of the mural and below them St. John supports Mary, the mother of Jesus. The sword piercing her heart symbolizes her grief, and at her feet Mary Magdalene kneels in sorrow. The recumbent figure of Jesus is at the center of the scene. Nicodemus leads the procession into the tomb. He is followed by St. Joseph of Arimathea, holding the legendary Holy Grail, the cup of the Last Supper that he is supposed to have taken to England. Jan Henrik de Rosen (1891–1982) painted the mural on the dry plaster using tempera on gold leaf. De Rosen used Cathedral

The Chapel of the Resurrection

The Chapel of the Resurrection, located directly beneath the south transept, is the clearest expression of the Norman style in the Cathedral. As such, it is believed to be the first structure of its type to be erected since the eleventh century. The chapel's architecture asserts the heavy, robust proportions, the semi-circular arches, and the more restrained degree of ornamentation that are all hallmarks of the Norman style.

The half-domed ceiling above the altar is embellished with a mosaic that portrays the Resurrection. The risen Christ, robed in white, bears in his hand the cross and banner of victory. Golden rays of the rising sun radiate against the iridescent turquoise sky behind him. At the right are two Roman soldiers, sleeping, while at the left an angel kneels before the open tomb. Hildreth Meiere (1892–1961), one of the few women artists represented in the Cathedral, designed the mosaic with a purity and cleanness of line that evokes the late art deco style of the 1920s and '30s. The entire altar area is framed by a chancel arch, which is composed of three concentric and distinct semi-circles. The wall behind the altar is a series of columns and interwoven arches. The needle-point kneelers repeat the motif of the interwoven arches and other symbols associated with the theme of Resurrection.

CASTING LIGHT AND GOOD

When Helen Keller died a few weeks before her eighty-eighth birthday, she left a legacy that had been fueled by her religious fervor and a dream "that every blind child have an opportunity to receive an education… and every blind adult, a chance for training and useful employment." With the support of a loving family, her dream did come true through her unceasing work in partnership with the American Foundation for the Blind and through her keen intellect and magnanimous warmth of personality that garnered the support of many.

At age nineteen months, as the result of illness, Keller was imprisoned in what she called a "no world" of blindness and deafness. With the help of her beloved teacher, Anne Sullivan Macy, at age eight she formed her first hand signals of sign language. In 1904, she graduated *cum laude* from Radcliffe College in Cambridge, Massachusetts. During this time, she wrote the first of eleven books she completed in her lifetime. Keller spoke seven languages and employed them as she lectured in thirty-five countries on five continents in pursuit of her dream. With boundless courage and faith, she not only made independent citizenship possible for the profoundly handicapped, she also fought vigorously against injustice, being one of the first to say that "the poor pay more" and labeling poverty as

"misery, degradation, blindness, crookedness and sin." In 1909, she became a member of the Socialist party and through it exercised her voice, especially when speaking of her abhorrence of war. The enactment of Social Security brought her the joy of seeing such "socialistic" programs active in her society. At age 75, Keller embarked on a 40,000-mile journey through Asia to promote services for the blind. Two years later, a similar mission took her to Scandinavian countries. As a witty and interesting conversationalist, she was admired by heads of state and the intellectuals of her day, including Albert Einstein, Mark Twain, and Alexander Graham Bell. Her commitment and faith served to bring about reforms that have become part of the American social structure.

Senator Lister Hill eulogized Helen Keller at her memorial service: "Although she was denied the light of day, Helen Keller cast more of the radiance of heaven than any person on this earth. Within this radiance and the light and example of her life, may we carry on in our troubled world…?"

When stitching begins to flow, you can almost meditate as you work. It's like playing a hymn that you're very familiar with.

—Luann Vaky
Needlepoint Committee, 1989

Six large recessed areas, four on the north wall and two on the west, or rear, wall, are each framed by an arch and adorned with mosaics depicting the post-Resurrection appearances of Christ. These mosaic panels are the work of Rowan and Irene LeCompte. Prior to this undertaking, the LeComptes had worked exclusively in the medium of stained glass. This underground setting, with the absence of daylight illumination, offered a unique challenge for artists fluent in the language of light. In preparation for the Resurrection Chapel mosaics, the couple spent a year in Istanbul, Turkey, studying mosaics by the Byzantine masters. The resulting six mosaics, with their glass tiles set at varying pitches, achieve the "spirited, colorful splendor" sought by architect Philip Frohman. Stylistically, the quality of abstraction suggests the sixth- and seventh-century Byzantine mosaics and painted icons, while reflecting the decorative abstraction popular during the 1960s, when these were created.

The mosaic closest to the sanctuary depicts the appearance of Jesus to Mary Magdalene. The second depicts His appearance to Cleopas and his wife Mary on the road to Emmaus. The next illustrates the risen Christ in the upper room surrounded by his disciples. The fourth mosaic shows Christ confronting doubting Thomas in the upper room. In the fifth, Christ appears to the disciples as they are fishing in the Sea of Tiberias. The sixth mosaic portrays the final appearance of the risen Christ, on the mountaintop described in the Gospels. There he charged his disciples to go into all the nations preaching and baptizing. Among the real people used as models to create the figures in this scene were Irene LeCompte, for whom the panel is a memorial, members of her family, and Cathedral architect Philip Frohman.

The chapel, which is reserved for prayer, serves as a memorial to the second Episcopal Bishop of Washington, the Right Reverend Alfred Harding, who is buried in the tomb at the base of the south pier supporting the chancel arch. The sarcophagus was designed by W. Douglas Caroe

(1857–1938), then resident architect of Canterbury Cathedral, and was carved from a single piece of limestone by the English sculptor Nathaniel Hitch (1846–1938). The figure of the bishop is presented as if he were sleeping, with a Bible loosely held in his left hand, open to the first verse of the Gospel of John. The carved figure of the bishop's bulldog rests against the bishop's feet and symbolizes fidelity.

The Cathedral Center for Prayer and Pilgrimage

Adjacent to the Chapel of the Resurrection, beneath the south transept porch, is the Cathedral Center for Prayer and Pilgrimage. The space has an unsettled history, having been designated, over the decades, as a sacristy, a security office, an embalming room, and, originally, a chapel dedicated to St. Dunstan, tenth-century Abbot of Glastonbury. Now the space provides hospitality and resources for persons seeking a quiet place to attend to their spiritual growth. Pillows, prayer bowls, candles, and icons, as well as books and journals, are available for use. The center is reserved for quiet prayer.

A small stained glass window provides the center's only natural illumination. The window features the image of St. Dunstan, tenth Archbishop of Canterbury, wearing his bishop's mitre and bearing a small organ and smith's tongs, emblems of his musical ability and his craftsmanship in metals. A second window, located in a nearby stairway inaccessible to the public, depicts St. Dunstan's coat of arms. These two windows are the first commissions received from the Cathedral by Rowan LeCompte, then a sixteen-year-old senior in high school. Over an astonishing career spanning more than six decades, LeCompte has created forty-eight windows and mosaics for the Cathedral and is the stained glass artist whose works occupy the greatest square footage. ■

The
Exterior

HERE ON AMERICAN SOIL is a soaring limestone structure, one of the largest churches in the world, that looks as
though it might be centuries old. In fact, Washington
National Cathedral was built entirely in the twentieth
century, and although it is a completely original design, it is
faithful to a much earlier style of architecture, one which
originated in France in the twelfth century, known as Gothic.

The dramatic innovations in building structure, techniques, and materials of the Gothic era transformed the
aesthetic possibilities of architecture, allowing it to serve as
a medium of expression of the spiritual aspirations of the age
in a new way. As never before, qualities of light and space
became essential elements of the interior and exterior design
of buildings. The dominant feature of Gothic architecture
was the pointed arch, which permitted the building of higher
walls and wider interior spaces. The introduction of flying
buttresses to the exterior to resist the lateral thrust of
arches and vaulted ceilings enabled walls to become, for the
first time, a building's "skin" rather than the primary bearers
of structural weight. With these elements in place, Gothic
cathedrals could be constructed to greater heights than ever
before. Walls became thinner, tall windows of stained

✜ *"SINCE MUSIC IS A VITAL PART OF THIS CATHEDRAL'S MINISTRY," CANON RICHARD FELLER WORKED WITH SCULPTOR JAY HALL CARPENTER TO BRING ANGEL MUSICIANS TO THE WEST TOWERS.*

glass replaced stone, and the effect of lightness and space intensified. More daylight reached the interior of the building and the color effects of the stained glass provided a supernatural atmosphere. These achievements, not purely technical, were immediately recognized for their ability to express spiritual truths. The Gothic idea was seen as lending material support to the spiritual aim of the Church in evangelizing the people. The twelfth-century French priest, Abbé Suger, considered one of the fathers of Gothic architecture, observed that stained glass windows had the power to "illumine men's minds so that they may attain an appreciation of God's light." So it is, also, eight hundred years later, with Washington National Cathedral. In fact, Bishop Satterlee, believing that no more appropriate architecture could be chosen for the Cathedral, is reputed to have said, "Gothic is God's style."

This sense of the "rightness" of Gothic has endured all the technical innovations of the intervening centuries and inspired the builders of Washington's Cathedral. The design of Washington National Cathedral closely

✜ *GABLET TERMINATIONS BECOME A HEAVENLY ORCHESTRA, WITH JAY HALL CARPENTER'S MUSICAL ANGELS.*

adheres to the English Gothic style of the fourteenth century, sometimes known as the Decorated or Middle Pointed style. "It was in the Fourteenth Century that Gothic Architecture in England attained its greatest beauty and perfection," Cathedral architect Philip Frohman wrote in a 1921 report to the Cathedral Chapter. He praised "the flower-like beauty of window tracery and the wealth of branch-like vaulting ribs" of this period and added a personal note that, had the Cathedral leaders chosen any other style, his own passion for the project would not have been as deep nor abiding.

✜ *A CURLEY-WHISKERED GARGOYLE AND FRIEND ON THE WEST SIDE OF THE SOUTH TRANSEPT, WITH THE WASHINGTON MONUMENT ENCIRCLED BY THE CITY, IN THE BACKGROUND*

The fundamental techniques used for building the Cathedral vary little from those used to build the great medieval cathedrals of Europe. The traditional methods of load-bearing masonry construction involved placing the limestone blocks one atop another with mortar between them. The force of gravity maintains the stability of the architecture. In a medieval cathedral the roof trusses were constructed from heavy timbers; the Cathedral builders opted for steel, for the sake of durability and fire safety.

The exterior of Washington National Cathedral reveals the grandeur of scale and perfection of detail that define Gothic architecture. The lofty and dominating central tower recalls the English cathedrals of Canterbury, Lincoln, and Gloucester; the two lower west towers invite comparison to those of York, Westminster Abbey, and Canterbury. The flying buttresses, the window tracery in the clerestory level, the canopied niches, the dozens of pinnacles, and the hundreds of carvings—grotesques and gargoyles, finials and crockets—all create patterns of light and shadow, add interest and softness, and imbue the heavy stones with a sense of lightness and verticality, a reaching toward heaven. With its balance of strength and delicate detail and in its equation of physical grace with spiritual grace, the Gothic style is achieved.

The Central Tower

In the early 1960s, Cathedral leaders, faced with limited funds, engaged in a major debate concerning whether to build the central tower to increase the visibility of the Cathedral or to extend the nave to provide seating for services. The former group prevailed and, in 1964, the Gloria in Excelsis Tower was dedicated, offering the entire city a

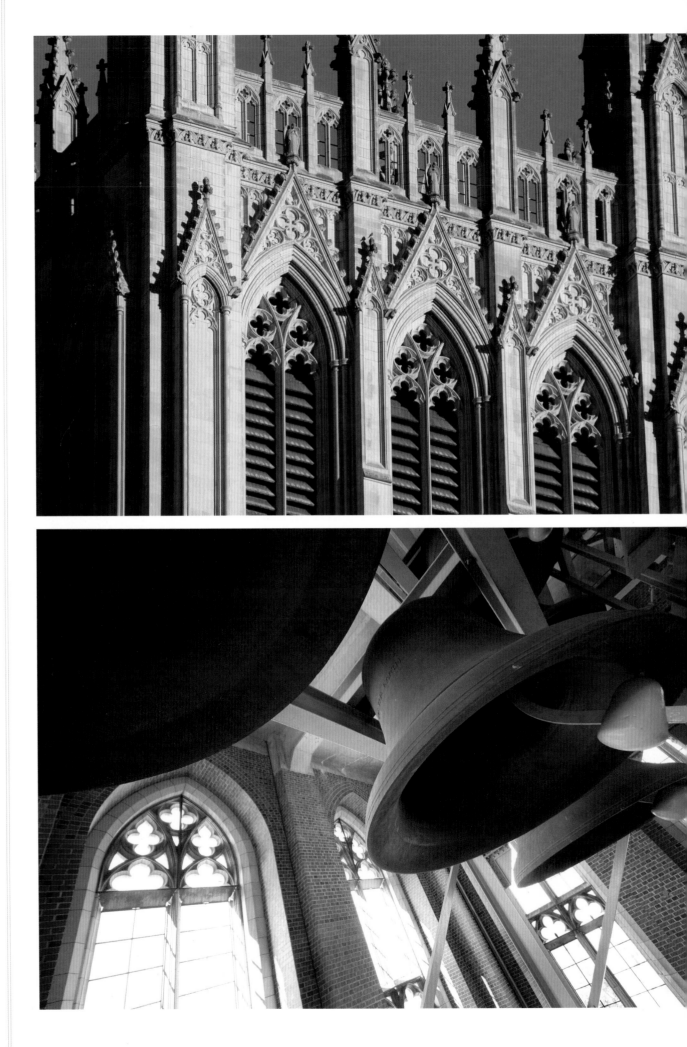

It has always been our aim that eventually the visitor to the Cathedral will behold it as a great book, reading its story in architecture, glass, and carving, and finding it a unified whole of which each bit is a related chapter or paragraph.

—DEAN FRANCIS B. SAYRE, JR., 1961

✢ TOP: THE DELICATE STONEWORK OF THESE GOTHIC TOWERS BELIE THE ORIGINS OF THIS ARCHITECTURAL STYLE'S NAME, TAKEN FROM THE BARBARIC GOTHS.

✢ BOTTOM: A GIFT OF FAITH FROM BESSIE J. KIBBEY, WHO GAVE THE FUNDS FOR THE CATHEDRAL'S CARRILLON FORTY-TWO YEARS BEFORE THE GLORIA IN EXCELSIS TOWER WAS BUILT

majestic and compelling image of the growing Gothic cathedral.

The tower rises 300 feet above the ground, rendering it taller than any of the medieval English cathedrals and, in modern terms, as tall as a thirty-story building. Arrayed on the tower are turrets, known as pinnacles, that taper upward to the top and bring the building's vertical appearance to a culmination. The four magnificent pinnacles, eight middle-sized balustrade pinnacles, and twenty-four small balustrade pinnacles are decorated with almost 400 carved angel figures, symbolizing the Seraphim and Cherubim surrounding the throne of God. These graceful winged carvings adorn every angle of intersection, as well as a frieze course positioned just beneath the top balustrade. Around the frieze, which is unique among Gothic cathedrals, are carved ninety-six angel likenesses, each with a different face.

The Cathedral features subtle and often unnoticed architectural refinements that might, in the crudest sense, be described as technical "imperfections" but which actually contribute to the visual perfection of the structure as a whole. The central tower is one such instance. With its west side one foot higher than its east side, the tower is not perfectly square. This and other deliberate adjustments forfend the harshness, rigidity, and mechanical quality that afflict most commercial buildings; instead, these adjustments endow the structure with qualities of grace and lightness, giving it, in the words of architect Philip Frohman, "that charm which we find in a beautiful freehand drawing."

In addition to its visual claim of pre-eminence on the Washington horizon, the central tower of the Cathedral also

makes its voice heard throughout the neighboring area: It is the only church in North America that houses both a ten-bell peal and a carillon in a single tower. The sixty-three bells, installed in 1963, were cast in English foundries, the ten-bell peal in the venerable Whitechapel Bell Foundry in London, and the fifty-three-bell, or four-and-one-half octaves, carillon in the Taylor Bell Foundry of Loughborough. At sixty-four tons in total weight, the Cathedral's Kibbey Carillon (a gift from Cathedral benefactor Bessie Kibbey) is the third heaviest in the world. The smallest bell weighs seventeen pounds and the largest weighs twelve tons.

Each of the carillon bells is connected by a taut steel cable to the clavier (keyboard), which is nestled in the tower amid the larger bells. When played, the clavier activates the metal clappers to strike the insides of the stationary bells. Directly above the Kibbey Carillon, the ten-bell peal set is mounted on a circular steel frame and controlled by means of ropes from the room beneath. Peal bells do not produce melodic music, but rather mathematical patterns of notes. The ringers, each assigned to a particular bell, pull the ropes that rotate the 608- to 3,588-pound bells. The Cathedral has two bands of ringers: the Washington Ringing Society, composed of adult volunteers, and the Whitechapel Guild of the National Cathedral School for Girls.

The North Porch and the Garth

The north transept entrance, with its vaulted porch, was the first completed entrance to the main level of the Cathedral. The Women's Porch, as it is known, honors the work of Christian women. The tympanum over the transept door represents St. Mary and the Christ Child, flanked on the left by two shepherds and on the right by the Magi standing in adoration. Directly beneath, in the trumeau niche, is a statue of St. Anne, mother of Mary. Niche statues in the exterior walls of the porch portray, from left to right, St.

Elizabeth, the mother of St. John the Baptizer; Mary Magdalene; St. Agnes; St. Cecilia; St. Monica, mother of St. Augustine of Hippo; St. Hilda, the Abbess of Whitby; and St. Catherine of Siena.

A cloister connects the north transept and its porch to the Cathedral's offices. Yet another cloister connects the apse with the office building and houses a rehearsal room for the choirs and music offices. The tranquil enclosure formed by the angle of these two cloisters and the Cathedral itself is called the garth. The large fountain in the center of the garth is the work of sculptor George Tsutakawa (1910–1997). The abstract Japanese design, with its free-flowing curved sheets and planes of silicone bronze, is intended to contrast with this English Gothic Cathedral.

✤ *The Angel Gabriel in a niche above the south portal, God's messenger traditionally portrayed with a scroll at the Annunciation*

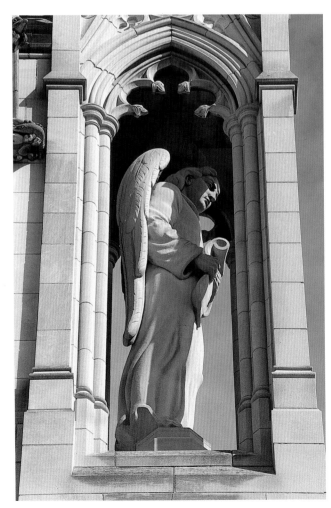

The Apse

At the east end of the Cathedral is the apse, the polygonal termination of the sanctuary. Completed in 1917, it is clearly visible between the soaring arches of the flying buttresses that support it. The figures of the saints Peter, John, and Paul, set in niches at the clerestory level, gaze toward the east, from whence each prophesied that the Christ would come again. The words inscribed on the frieze below the apse parapet are the angel's chorus from the Revelation to John: "Alleluia, The Lord God Omnipotent Reigneth, Alleluia." With these figures and inscription, the meticulously planned iconographic scheme of the Cathedral is completed, as they represent the last book of the New Testament, the Revelation to John, and the expectation of Christ coming again.

The South Portal

In the highest portion of the south transept façade, where the massive architecture yields to more lacy forms, there are two majestic angelic figures set in the tall, fully-canopied niches flanking the rose window. The eight-foot-tall figures are the Archangels Gabriel and Michael, sculpted by Granville Carter (1920–1992), carved by Paul Palumbo (1923–1997), and installed in 1962.

The theme of the tympanum above the south transept portal is the Last Supper, a subject never before depicted over a cathedral doorway. The figure of Christ stands within the curve of the table, surrounded by his disciples in various positions of supplication. With his arms outstretched and holding the bread and wine, he beckons, "Come unto me all who labor and are heavy laden, and I will refresh you." Three scenes from the story of the Emmaus Road are carved in panels beneath. Sculpted by Heinz Warneke, the carving of the tympanum took two years to complete.

Directly beneath the tympanum, in a niche between the doors, is a large statue of St. Alban (ca. 305), the first British martyr. On each side of the massive oak doors, eight carved figures of biblical characters, the work of Spanish sculptor Enrique Monjo (1895–1976), stand as witnesses to the scene above. The figures represent the many whose lives were touched by the earthly life of Jesus. They are, on the east side of the door, the widow who gave her mite; the sick spirit; Lazarus; and blind Bartimaeus;

✤ *Saints Peter, Paul, and John greet the rising sun each day from their niches beneath the Apse windows.*

and, on the west side, the boy with loaves and fishes; Nicodemus; the woman by the well; and Judas Iscariot.

Forty-four carved figures of angels, arrayed on the archivolt in four concentric arcs, span the perimeter of the pointed arch, which shelters the south entrance. The rows of angels, who guard the throne of God, are witness to the divinity of Christ. Enrique Monjo created the plaster models for the figures, each of which is different. Roger Morigi and Frank Zic devoted four-and-a-half years to carving the niche figures. Both the angels and their intricate canopies, designed by architect Frohman, were carved in place.

The West Towers

The west façade, sometimes called the west front, consists of two towers, a gallery halfway down, a rose window, and three grand portals, each with a large tympanum carved above. Both the north and south towers, respectively known as the St. Peter and St. Paul towers, rise 232 feet in height. More than 2,700 carved stones complete the two towers with their eight great pinnacles, sixteen intermediate pinnacles, 128 carved dentils, and many other decorative stones. A finial in the St. Paul Tower was set in place on September 29, 1990, to mark the completion of the Cathedral, eighty-three years to the day from the setting of the first stone.

More than a dozen carvers worked on the hundreds of angels that embellish the west towers. When sculptor Jay Hall Carpenter (b. 1959) was asked to design them, he proposed that each one hold or play a musical instrument. To avoid what he called "the stereotypical angel," Carpenter carved the angels to represent many races, male and female. Some of the angel musicians are personal commemorations requested by their donors: An angel with cymbals is in gratitude for a spouse's recovery from cancer; another with a trumpet honors a classmate killed in the Vietnam War; one with hand bells celebrates the honoree's birthday; and the one holding an Academy Award is a tribute by the stone carvers to the filmmaker Marjorie Hunt, whose documentary chronicling their work earned her the award.

The Cathedral Close

The land on which the Cathedral stands is known as the Close. The fifty-nine acres feature three schools, a center for learning and spiritual development, a formal garden, and a woodland area.

In 1907, as ground was broken for the construction of the Cathedral, Frederick Law Olmsted, Jr. (1870–1957), was appointed to design the Cathedral gardens and grounds. One

✤ CARVERS ROGER MORIGI AND FRANK ZIC SPENT FOUR-AND-A-HALF YEARS CREATING SCULPTOR ENRIQUE MONJO'S FIGURES OF THE SAINTS AND ANGELS IN THE SOUTH PORTAL.

CURIOUS CREATURES

The exterior of Washington National Cathedral is teeming with inhabitants, from the lowest ledges where gargoyles dwell, to the highest pinnacles, where angels soar. These stone beings take their origin from painted fanciful figures of intermixed animal, human, and plant forms found on the walls of ancient Roman rooms known as *groteschi,* and are called grotesques. Gargoyles are a subcategory of this group and are most readily associated with Gothic architecture. The primary root for the word gargoyle is the Latin *gargula,* meaning "gullet." The word is also related to the French verb *gargariser* meaning "to gargle." Grotesques serve the very practical purpose of carrying water away from the Cathedral through either a channel along their top or through a pipe from

within (gargoyles). Were these fantastic creatures not in place, water would erode masonry, create dampness inside the Cathedral, and destroy the structure's foundation.

The grotesques that dwell on the exterior of Washington National Cathedral are not only traditional types of beings and creatures, but also ones that are notably American and others that capture people and events from the life of this city and of the Cathedral. The *Wisconsin Badger* can be found on the exterior north nave, bay two, triforium level, east gargoyle. On the southwest tower perches the horned *Crooked Politician* that holds the scale of justice, obviously out of balance. There are grotesques of master stone

carvers who wrangled these spirited stones into existence: Vincent Palumbo, Constantine Seferlis, Gino Bresciani, and Patrick Plunkett. *Flirtatious Stone Carver* and *Aghast Dean* (above) were inspired by the story of a young single stone carver's flirtations with women passing by the Cathedral. One bright, sunny day, the carver was caught by an appalled Dean Francis Sayre, Jr. *Flirtatious Stone Carver* is posed hanging from scaffolding, winking, and whistling. *Aghast Dean* is captured as an angelically winged, robed priest carrying his Bible, his face frozen in horror and surprise. Probably the most famous of the grotesques is the villainous *Darth Vader* from the movie Star Wars, who was suggested by Chris Rader, in a "name the grotesque" contest. Mr. Rader, then only thirteen years old, felt that *Darth Vader* best met the criteria for a modern-day grotesque, being a character of monstrous and demonic spirit. *Darth Vader* is located on the dark, north side of the Cathedral.

A theory as to the origin of grotesques is that they were intended to increase attendance in the early Christian church by luring those who had worshiped similar creatures in local religions that preceded and, for a time, coexisted with the early church.

of America's foremost landscape architects, Olmsted was known for his design of the National Mall and the grounds of the White House, among other Washington projects. Of the Cathedral assignment, Olmsted wrote: "The great charm of approaching the Cathedral through and up a wooded hillside, leaving the city far behind and below, helping one to forget the hurly-burly and busy-ness of a work-a-day world must be taken advantage of to the fullest extent... So that one at last reaches the Cathedral cleansed in mind and spirit." The first master plan for the Close, which Olmsted completed in 1910, sought to enhance the site's unique elements, particular-ly its panoramic vistas of the city, the undulating topography, and the extensive natural woodlands.

On the northeast side of the Cathedral is the Cathedral Col-lege. Founded in 1929 as the Col-lege of Preachers to provide post-ordination training to clergy, it is the oldest institution of its kind in the United States. In 2004, the College of Preachers and Washington National Cathedral merged their educational programs to form the Cathedral College.

Throughout the academic year, the col-lege offers intensive post-graduate training to clergy and operates a lay academy with a broad range of educational programs. Speakers have included world faith leaders, such as the Reverend Billy Graham, Arch-bishop Desmond Tutu, and the Dalai Lama. Also, the college has presented spe-cial programs and events, devoted to spe-cific topics, among these Sacred Circles, a conference to explore the spirituality of women; Breakthrough: The Women, Faith, and Development Summit to End Global Poverty; and the Martin Luther King Youth Non-Violence Day.

CARVERS OF STONE

To be called a stone carver is to be acknowledged as a member of a profession that encapsulates the legacy of a small culture. Stone carv-ing is a tradition of place, craftsmen originating from places in the world where stone is found that possesses the strength for monumental structures, yet the grain and texture that allows intricate carving. Stone carving is also a tradition of family. Children of master carvers often become apprentices who carry on the family trade. Within this family tradition is passed every nuance of the craft, from the knowledge acquired from day-to-day work in the fam-ily carver's shed to the aptitude for being a craftsman and an artist

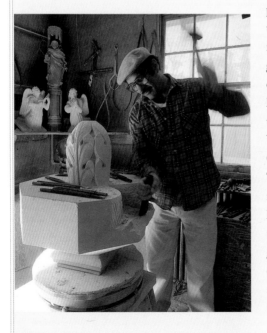

pulling from ridged stone the subtle, lyrical line that forms the snarl of a gargoyle or the exquisite elegance of the human form found on the west façade of Washington National Cathedral in *Ex Nihilo*. To this magnificent manipulation of stone by human hands and heart the stone carver brings great pride and the gift of an artwork that will astound and give pleasure to generations of viewers.

To the south of the college, facing the Cathedral apse, is a library housing the collections of several distinguished cler-gy. The first wing was completed in 1927 with a gift of the late Mrs. Violet Blair Janin in memory of her mother, Mary Jesup Blair. Built of brick with limestone trim, it is similar to one of the library buildings at Cambridge University. Adjoin-ing this wing at a right angle is the second addition, which was opened in 1952 as a memorial to Colonel Lorenzo Sitgreaves and Lucy Jesup Sitgreaves.

Sayre House, on the far side of the south roadway, once served as the resi-dence of the Cathedral dean and now houses offices for Cathedral staff.

On the southwest side of the Cathe-

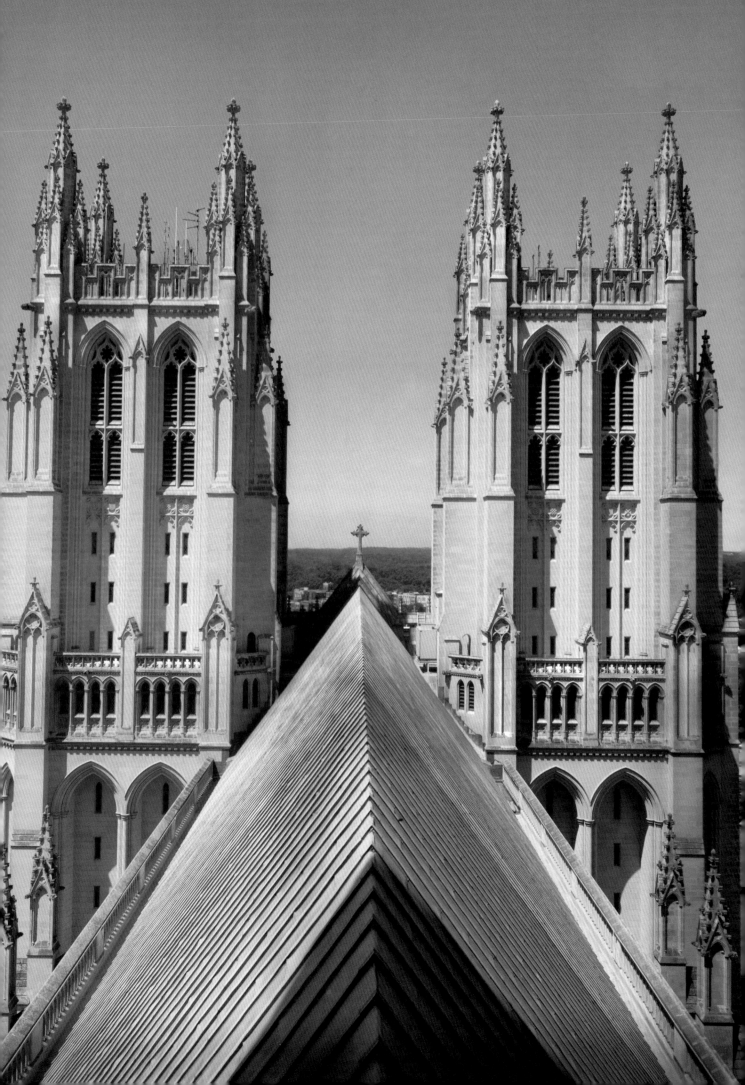

dral is the Tudor-style Episcopal Church House, originally known as the Bishop's House. Constructed in 1913, for many years it served as the family residence of the diocesan bishop. In the 1950s, the interior of Episcopal Church House was remodeled, creating a headquarters for the Episcopal Diocese of Washington, a function which continues today. The house contains the Chapel of the Annunciation, which commemorates twenty women, one for each century since the birth of Christ, who made major contributions to the Christian tradition. The sanctuary is dominated by the eastern window, which, with its brilliant reds and blues, depicts the Annunciation. The remaining stained glass windows portray the Christian women. Members of altar guilds throughout the Diocese of Washington created the kneelers and seat cushions.

Also on the Close are the three schools that fulfill the Cathedral's charter, enacted by Congress, which called "for the promotion of religion, education and charity." Boys and girls attend the Beauvoir School from nursery school through third grade. The National Cathedral School for Girls, which opened in 1900, offers instruction from grades four through twelve. Likewise, St. Albans School, established in 1909, provides instruction to boys in grades four through twelve. Boys and girls of both schools who earn music scholarships sing in the Cathedral Choirs.

Continuing the Legacy

The placing of the finial stone atop the St. Paul Tower in 1990 marked the completion of the Cathedral, but only in the structural sense. Throughout the Cathedral, portions of the decorative fabric remain unfinished, awaiting the imprimatur of future generations. These stone carving projects include the triforium spandrels in the great choir, the north transept high vaulting bosses, a number of north and south aisle vaulting bosses, and the six life-size niche figures for the central portal of the west façade. In the case of the choir spandrels, the desire to open a section of the Cathedral for worship mitigated against the urge to complete carvings. At every stage of its construction, the Cathedral has balanced competing needs of funds, manpower, and timing. These logistical compromises have created opportunities for future generations, who can participate in the continuing visual expression of faith that is the Cathedral.

The Bishop's Garden and the Herb Cottage

In 1916, Florence Brown Bratenahl (1884–1940), wife of the Cathedral's second dean and a landscape artist and gardener who had trained with Olmsted, established All Hallows Guild, a volunteer organization dedicated to maintaining and beautifying the Cathedral grounds. Bratenahl succeeded Olmsted as the Cathedral's landscape designer when he left in 1928. Among her projects were the designs of the Bishop's Garden, the Pilgrim Steps, and the courtyard and gardens for the building then known as the College of Preachers.

Bratenahl's first focus was the Bishop's Garden, which is located on the south side of the Cathedral. Under her direction, the garden was laid out, mature specimens of boxwood, yew, holly, and other historical trees and flowers planted, and places of quiet refuge created that were embellished with sculptures and ancient artifacts and furnishings. The Bishop's Garden was formally dedicated in 1928. Today, it continues to be the place of "holy stillness" that Bratenahl envisioned.

From the outset, the designers of the Cathedral grounds, like the architects of the Cathedral itself, sought to incorporate elements that enriched not only the beauty of the Close but also its spiritual and historic fabric. To that end, plants with historical associations were included: heirloom boxwood from Dolly Madison's inaugural bouquet and trees from George Washington's Mount Vernon and Thomas Jefferson's Monticello. Likewise, plants and artifacts from sacred sites brought symbolic value: trees from the Holy Land and relics from monasteries and abbeys.

A memorial replica of a twelfth-century Norman arch marks the entrance to the walled garden. From there, a curving, stone-paved path leads to the garden's inner entrance, known as the Norman Court after its central feature, a twelfth-century arch found at a ruined monastery. Two tall

❧ *"A Wayside Cross, centuries old, marking this garden's dedication, its spirit is felt by all who enter within this fragrant stillness…"*
—Florence Bratenahl

The great charm of approaching the Cathedral through and up a wooded hillside, leaving the city far behind and below, helping one to forget the hurly-burly, and busy-ness of a work-a-day world must be taken advantage of to the fullest extent... So that one at last reaches the Cathedral cleansed in mind and in spirit.

—FREDERICK LAW OLMSTED, JR.
Cathedral landscape architect, 1919

Atlas blue cedars brought from the Holy Land in 1901 and planted as foot-tall saplings flank the Norman Court.

A number of the medieval artifacts in the Bishop's Garden, including the Norman arch, were given by or purchased from sculptor George Gray Barnard (1863–1938), who was a close friend of the Bratenahls. As a young man, Barnard had traveled throughout the countryside of southern France. The collection of medieval art that grew out of those early travels eventually formed the core of The Cloisters of the Metropolitan Museum of Art in New York. Elsewhere in the garden are other ancient artifacts from Barnard's travels: two stone capitals, one forming the base of a sundial and the other a shallow water bowl for birds; five bas-reliefs, set into walls that enclose the garden; and the Wayside Cross, a boundary marker used to guide early Christian pilgrims.

Bratenahl incorporated within the Bishop's Garden a medieval-style herb garden, known as the Hortulus ("little garden"), planted with herbs found on a list drawn up by Charlemagne in 812 CE. The centerpiece of the herb garden is a ninth-century Carolingian font, the oldest of the Cathedral's freestanding and intact artifacts. This font, also one of Barnard's acquisitions, was originally from the Abbey of St. Julie in Aisne, France. Other elements of the Bishop's Garden include the Shadow House, constructed with stones from President Cleveland's summer home, the Bishop's Lawn, two perennial gardens, and a rose garden. On a more contemporary note, the granite statue of the Prodigal Son provides a focal point to the rose walk. Sculpted and carved by Heinz Warneke, the work is striking for its low relief and simplicity.

Adjacent to the garden, on its northwest side, is the Herb Cottage, a project of All Hallows Guild. The octagonal structure, one of the oldest buildings on the Close, was originally built as the baptistery for the Cathedral, but has for many decades housed a gift shop, the proceeds of which fund maintenance and improvements to the gardens and grounds.

Olmsted Woods and the Pilgrim Steps

On the east side of the Bishop's Garden, a set of fifty-one broad steps, called the Pilgrim Steps, leads from the south transept of the Cathedral downward to Olmsted Woods and to an heroic bronze statue, by Herbert Haseltine (1877–1962), of George Washington on horseback. The steps, designed by Florence Bratenahl and given to the Cathedral by Roland Taylor, are constructed of stone from a quarry originally owned and operated by George Washington. The statue presents Washington as a young man with a mature, strong face.

The five-acre Olmsted Woods is one of the few old-growth forests still standing in Washington. In the mid-1990s, All Hallows Guild embarked on a restoration of the Woods, restoring soil, planting native plants, removing invasive exotics, encouraging wildlife, adding a series of walkways, and refurbishing the Woodland Bridge. The recent restoration of an original outdoor amphitheater at the edge of the woods provides a terraced site for convocation, services, and pilgrimages. ■

TOP: IN THE EARLY DAYS OF CATHEDRAL WORSHIP, THIS RECENTLY RESTORED AMPHITHEATER WAS THE SITE OF OPEN-AIR SERVICES TO WHICH SOMETIMES THOUSANDS OF PEOPLE WOULD COME.

BOTTOM: HERBERT HASELTINE'S GEORGE WASHINGTON SEEMS TO BE TURNED TOWARDS THE CATHEDRAL RISING ABOVE PILGRIM ROAD.

Building the Cathedral

"Godspeed in the work begun this noon," declared President Theodore Roosevelt to a gathering of thousands, on September 29, 1907, at the laying of the Foundation Stone of Washington National Cathedral. The Right Reverend Henry Yates Satterlee, first Episcopal Bishop of Washington, placed the mortar on the block of American granite, in which was embedded a smaller stone from a field near Bethlehem. Laid beneath what would become Bethlehem Chapel, the block of granite bore the inscription: "The Word was made flesh, and dwelt among us" (John 1:14). These words were a statement of the iconography of the enormous project which lay ahead, affirmed the devotion of the people who undertook it, and provided in a single phrase the message it was dedicated to communicating with the world. With the point of a ceremonial sterling silver trowel, Satterlee drew the sign of the cross in the mortar and thus began one

✤ *LABORERS WORKING*
ON THE OVERCROFT
AND ROOF OF THE NORTH
TRANSEPT IN 1932

of the most extended "acts of optimism," as the modern architect Le Corbusier once described the great medieval cathedrals, of the twentieth century.

With the laying of the Foundation Stone, the grassy, tree-shrouded Close became home to the longest running construction site in the history of the nation's capital. As with medieval cathedrals, construction of the Cathedral occurred in phases of steady work interrupted by periods of little progress that were the result of war, or more often, the lack of funding to continue construction. The process took a full eighty-three years. Some of the great medieval churches were built more quickly, but some took significantly longer. All of the funds used to build the Cathedral,

✚ The opening procession during the laying of the Foundation Stone, September 29, 1907

and which maintain it today, came, and continue to come, from private donations, and not from any local nor federal government nor from any national church.

For eight decades, then, the drive to build a Gothic cathedral in the nation's capital withstood forces, historic and financial, that halted construction for five different periods and consistently threatened the completion of this sustained and collective act of faith. The periods of struggle—deaths of bishops and deans and architects, two world wars, the Great Depression, crippling inflation, the rise of secularism, competition for limestone, and severe debt—also included moments of celebration, be they the dedication of a memorial bay or the completion of a rose window. Progress was driven by the optimism, patience, perseverance, and belief in divine providence of thousands of Cathe-

✠ BISHOP HENRY YATES
SATTERLEE, FIRST
BISHOP OF WASHINGTON

dral supporters, craftspeople, artists, clergy, and benefactors. Many understood that the vision of a completed Cathedral would not be realized in their lifetimes, but that they were collaborating in an endeavor larger than any one individual and one that would require the faithful contributions of not only individuals but also generations.

Plans for building Washington National Cathedral gained momentum largely through the efforts of Episcopal leaders, such as the Rev. George Douglas and the Rev. Randolph McKim, who sought assistance from Washington community leaders, such as Riggs Bank President Charles C. Glover. On January 6, 1893, Congress granted the charter allowing the Protestant Episcopal Cathedral

✠ A 1923 AERIAL VIEW OF
THE CATHEDRAL UNDER
CONSTRUCTION SHOWS ITS
FINAL OUTLINE.

Foundation (PECF) of the District of Columbia to establish a cathedral and institutions of higher learning.

At that time, Episcopal churches in the District of Columbia were part of the Diocese of Maryland. Those who had organized the movement to build a cathedral pressed for a separate diocese. In May 1895, with the support of Bishop William Paret, sixth Bishop of Maryland, and the consent of the Episcopal Diocese of Maryland, the Episcopal Diocese of Washington was created, consisting of the District of Columbia and four neighboring Maryland counties.

Henry Yates Satterlee was consecrated as Washington's first Episcopal bishop in March 1896, and he immediately began the search for a cathedral site. He found it on Mount St. Alban, a stunning thirty-acre tract of land in the northwest corner of the city. (Eventually, the Cathedral Close

would encompass fifty-seven acres.) Satterlee later wrote, "I shall never forget the sensations with which at the board meeting I took up the pen to sign the contract for the purchase of the Cathedral property. It required as much nerve and courage as I have ever put forth." Some criticized Satterlee for selecting a spot so remote from what was then the city's center. Their concern was that few would travel so far to worship. But the bishop, a native of New York City, understood that cities grow and that the Cathedral would not remain isolated for long.

Bishop Satterlee envisioned the Cathedral, perched on one of Washington's highest elevations, becoming a national beacon, "a ceaseless witness for Jesus Christ and His Incarnation." He also envisioned the Cathedral as a "house of prayer for all people." Taken from the Book of Isaiah 56:7, this concept has been central to the Cathedral's identity and mission from its earliest days.

Grounding Satterlee's vision of a great Gothic cathedral in the nation's capital was the recognition that he could not accomplish this task alone and that neither the newly created Episcopal Diocese of Washington nor the local community would be able to provide sufficient funds. Well-known and well-traveled, Satterlee turned to his prominent friends

in the wider Episcopal Church, asking for their support. The committees established by Satterlee in Philadelphia, New York, and Boston were the founding chapters of what would become the National Cathedral Association, the basis of a national network of friends of the Cathedral.

In 1906, the Cathedral Chapter voted to build the Cathedral in a style of architecture which developed in thirteenth- and fourteenth-century England and became known as the Decorated Gothic. They chose as the Cathedral's first architects Englishman George Frederick Bodley (1847–1907), the pre-eminent Gothic architect of his time, and American Henry Vaughan (1845–1917), a Boston architect, born in England, who had trained under Bodley.

Although the Foundation Stone had been laid in 1907, the actual construction did not begin until 1910. During the interim, Cathedral leaders searched for the ideal type of building stone. Finally, the Building Committee, assisted by geologists, endorsed Indiana oolitic limestone, primarily for its adaptability to hand carving. The characteristic is important for Gothic structures because they incorporate a plethora of intricate carvings, such as gargoyles. Indiana oolitic limestone is relatively soft and easily cut when first quarried, but hardens during prolonged exposure to air, enhancing the lifespan of whatever form it takes. Also, this stone has remarkable texture, which facilitates carving. Furthermore, because it is more elastic than many types of building stone, it withstands sudden changes in temperature that cause less flexible stone to crack and crumble.

Following medieval tradition, construction of Washington National Cathedral began at the east end, where the

83 YEARS LATER

WITH THE INSPIRED DETERMINATION AND THE CONSTANT FUNDRAISING EFFORTS OF SIX BISHOPS AND SEVEN DEANS, CONSTRUCTION OF THE CATHEDRAL SPANNED TWO WORLD WARS AND A DEPRESSION BEFORE IT WAS COMPLETED IN 1990.

1909

1926

1939

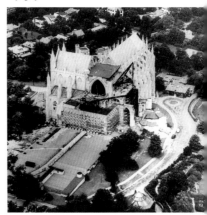

High Altar is situated, and progressed westward, like the path of the sun. (This tradition probably evolved from forms of pre-Christian worship that faced eastward toward Jerusalem and the rising sun.) After the completed Bethlehem Chapel was dedicated in 1912, construction ceased for three years, resuming in 1915 with the apse, which was completed in 1919. Because of the lack of funding following World War I, construction was suspended in 1919 for two years.

In 1921, following the deaths of Bodley and Vaughan, the Cathedral contracted with the Boston architectural firm of Frohman, Robb & Little. For the next fifty years, Philip Hubert Frohman refined, revised, and completed the plans of Bodley and Vaughan into a unified architectural masterpiece, incorporating elements of the French and Spanish Gothic styles into the design and creating an amalgam of the finest Gothic architecture. Described as a "Gothic genius," Frohman had begun serious study of medieval cathedral architecture at the age of eleven, and recognized the job of completing the design of Washington National Cathedral as the opportunity of a lifetime. Frohman's erudition, sense of balance, and good judgement, made something new within a profound reverence for tradition. When Frohman retired in 1971, virtually all the architectural drawings for the Cathedral were complete. Howard B. Trevillian, Jr. (d. 1993), Frohman's chief draftsman, carried out Frohman's vision as superintending architect until 1981,

1962

1971

1981

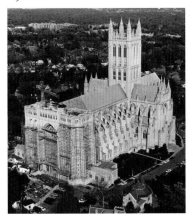

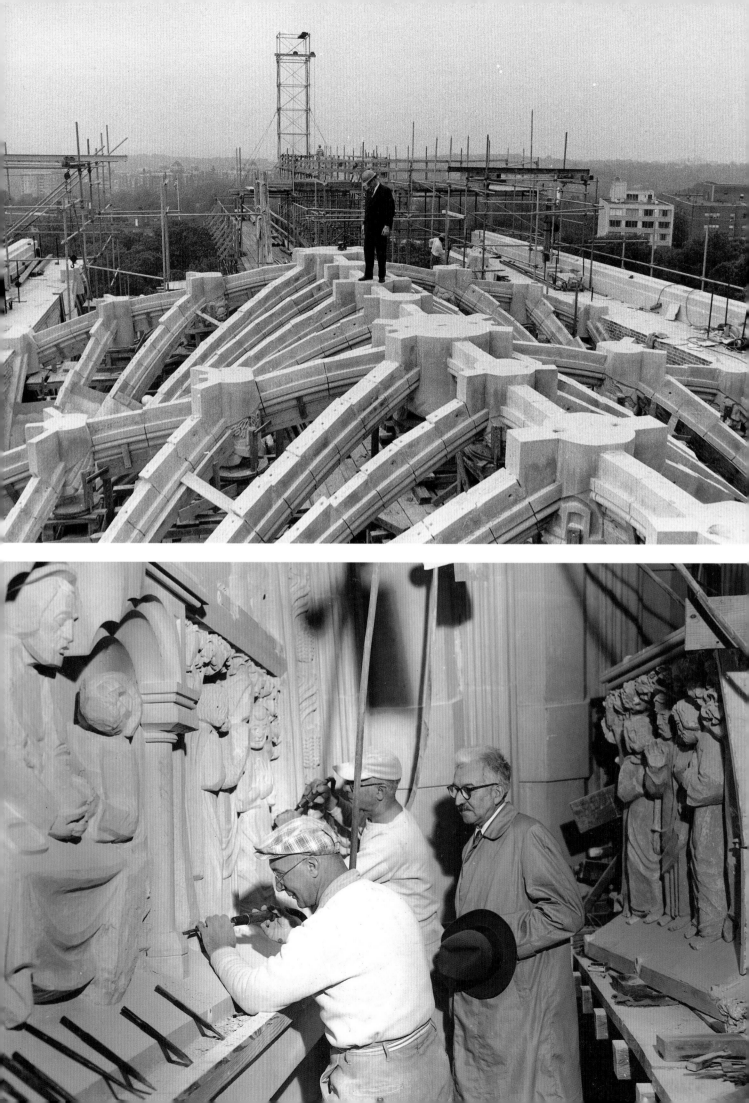

✤ *Philip H. Frohman*
(l.), the Cathedral's
chief architect for
fifty years, and Dean
Francis B. Sayre, Jr.
(r.), its second iconog-
rapher, worked
together more than
twenty years.

after which the firm of Smith, Segreti & Tepper oversaw the final years of construction.

The first major phase of construction under Frohman's direction, from 1922 until 1941, included the completion of the great choir and north transept and the construction of one-third of the south transept. Following the 1929 stock market crash and the ensuing Depression, fundraising efforts were less successful, but work moved forward in a series of very small contracts that maintained the pool of talented artisans who had been assembled and provided jobs to men who might otherwise have been on the bread lines. The north transept, begun in 1930, was not completed until 1941.

✤ Top: *Canon Richard*
Feller, Cathedral
Clerk of the Works
for almost forty
years, stands atop the
clerestory vaulting of
the nave in 1969.

✤ Bottom: *Sculptor*
Heinz Warneke
observes carvers Roger
Morigi (front) and
Edward Ratti (back)
as they bring to life
Warneke's sculpture
of the south portal
tympanum.

World War II brought a shortage of funds and of workers. In 1942, just after the completion of the north porch, construction was halted and did not resume until 1948. The next nine years of work allowed for the completion of the lower two-thirds of the south transept and the beginning of the nave. In 1957, owing to lack of funds, construction was halted for a fourth time. With the receipt of a large bequest, construction recommenced in 1960 and continued, uninterrupted, for an unprecedented seventeen years.

In 1962 work began on the 300-foot Gloria in Excelsis central tower. The decision by the Cathedral Chapter to build the central tower instead of completing the nave was strongly influenced by Dean Francis B. Sayre, Jr., who felt that the sight of the magnificent tower high above the city would inspire the private donations upon which the Cathedral depended. "The tower will build the nave," he asserted. In his twenty-seven years as dean, serving from 1951 to 1978, Sayre was a guiding force in all aspects of the construction of the Cathedral. Also during his watch, the development of the icono-graphic scheme introduced by the Cathedral's second dean, George C. F. Bratenahl, was finalized.

The Gloria in Excelsis tower

✤ *The Cathedral is*
completed with the
laying of the 1,008-
pound finial atop the
National Cathedral
Association pinnacle
on St. Paul Tower on
September 29, 1990.

was dedicated in 1964. As Dean Sayre had predicted, donations did materialize for completion of the nave. In 1976, the Cathedral's nave was dedicated in the presence of Queen Elizabeth II, President Gerald Ford, and thousands of others.

After such a productive term, which had seen the completion of the south transept, the central tower, the nave, and two-thirds of the west front, work was suspended again, in 1977, and all but two stone carvers let go, with no idea when, or if, work would resume again. That same year John T. Walker was installed as the sixth Bishop of Washington; a year later, he assumed the additional title of Dean of the Cathedral. The following year, in 1980, Walker, assisted by Cathedral Provost Charles A. Perry, launched a capital campaign to retire a debt that exceeded $10 million. Simultaneously, Walker pursued other goals: the completion of the unfinished observation gallery and the retention of enough skilled craftspeople to finish the twin towers of the west façade. Building resumed in 1980 and the Pilgrim Observation Gallery opened to the public in 1982. The final phase of construction began the following year. That decade of work, from 1980 to 1990, brought the completion of the towers of St. Peter (north) and St. Paul (south) and of the west façade, with sculptor Frederick

Hart's expressive representation of creation in its central tympanum. In ceremonies attended by President George H. W. Bush and several people who had been present as children at the laying of the Foundation Stone, the last stone (the National Cathedral Association finial) was set atop the St. Paul Tower and Washington National Cathedral was completed. "It was like putting the last gem in Christ's crown," master mason Billy Cleland said of the historic moment. The date was September 29, 1990, eighty-three years to the day from the laying of the Foundation Stone. ■

The Living Cathedral

Like living stones, let yourselves be built into a spiritual house. —1 Peter 2:5

As the Cathedral enters its second century of service, it is time for it to turn its great beauty outward. After eighty-three years of building what has become a spiritual home for the nation, the Cathedral serves as a voice for a generous-spirited, vigorous, and thoughtful Christian faith. Our Canterbury Pulpit provides the vehicle from which important truth-tellers address the nation, while our robust worship and programmatic life calls us to embody God's love and to welcome people of all faiths and none.

Within this sacred space and beyond the beautiful architecture and grounds featured in this guidebook, a diverse national community beckons us to engage in interfaith dialogue, to convene world leaders to address the pressing social and moral issues of our day, and to be a catalyst for reconciliation in our city, nation, and world.

This community is made up of people like you. The following pages illustrate the programs, lectures, worship, and events of national significance that take place here every year.

Whether in person or online, your National Cathedral community is what breathes life into this church and its work. People come to visit. They experience the profound beauty here and are inspired to act. We learn from each other and the great minds who join us in conversation about ways to heal this broken world. And all of us have a part to play in the Cathedral's next century of building, one where limestone is replaced by the living stones of God's people.

This cathedral is open to all seekers every day of the year. We hope you visit us often. ■

✣ *At the concluding service of the Cathedral's Centennial Year (2007-2008), Cathedral Dean Samuel T. Lloyd III challenged all "to look forward to the new century of ministry to which God beckons us."*

✤ THE NAVE OF WASHINGTON
NATIONAL CATHEDRAL CAME
ALIVE WITH SONG, COLOR,
MOVEMENT, AND JOYFUL
WORSHIP IN NOVEMBER 2006
AS THOUSANDS JOINED IN
THE INVESTITURE OF THE
26TH PRESIDING BISHOP OF
THE EPISCOPAL CHURCH,
KATHARINE JEFFERTS SCHORI.

✤ ABOVE: *A Cathedral Christmas tradition and a highlight of the liturgical year, Handel's Messiah brings together the combined Cathedral choirs and orchestra under the direction of Music Director Michael McCarthy.*

✤ LEFT: *Some one hundred Cathedral docents continue a tradition of welcome begun in the 1920s as they share the Cathedral's fabric and mission with more than 750,000 visitors annually.*

✤ RIGHT: *Acolytes from across the country join in the Cathedral's Acolyte Festival, a day-long celebration of dedication and faith.*

✦ ABOVE: *HUNDREDS*
GATHERED IN APRIL 2008
FOR A CATHEDRAL
EVENSONG IN MEMORY OF
THE VICTIMS OF THE
VIRGINIA TECH SLAYINGS.

✦ RIGHT: *MEMBERS*
OF NUMEROUS NATIVE
AMERICAN NATIONS PAR-
TICIPATE IN THE SERVICE
HONORING THE OPENING
OF THE SMITHSONIAN
INSTITUTION'S MUSEUM OF
THE AMERICAN INDIAN.

✤ ABOVE: *THE CATHEDRAL HONORS OTHER FAITH TRADITIONS' WAYS OF REACHING FOR THE SACRED. HERE, BUDDHIST MONKS CREATE A SAND MANDALA DURING THE INTERFAITH PEACE PRAYER PRACTICES EVENT IN OCTOBER 2007.*

✤ LEFT: *SOME REGULARLY ATTEND SERVICES AS PART OF THE CATHEDRAL CONGREGATION. SOME COME ON A TOUR, TO SEE A BEAUTIFUL CHURCH. SOME PAUSE IN THEIR DAILY ROUTINE FOR A BRIEF MOMENT WITH GOD. ALL ARE WELCOME.*

✢ *"Whoever shall not receive the kingdom of God as a little child, shall not enter therein." Whether taking part in an Easter service (top) or a Christmas pageant (right) or simply wondering at the beauty of this huge place (above), children continually remind us through their lively and genuine curiosity and enthusiasm of Jesus' admonition to reach for God's love with a simple faith.*

✣ AMID THE MAJESTY OF THE PIERS AND VAULTING, THE EXQUISITE BEAUTY OF THE SCULPTURE AND ARTWORK, THE CATHEDRAL REMEMBERS ITS PRIMARY MISSION, AS EXPRESSED BY CATHEDRAL DEAN SAMUEL T. LLOYD III, "TO WELCOME STRANGERS INTO OUR MIDST, AND INVITE THEM TO BECOME FELLOW PILGRIMS AND FRIENDS."

✢ Below: *In April 2008, the Cathedral present- ed "Breakthrough: The Women, Faith, and Development Summit to End Global Poverty," attended by thousands from around the world and co-chaired by former U.S. Secretary of State Madeleine Albright.*

✢ Left: *At the Cathedral's Sunday Forum, Cathedral Dean Samuel T. Lloyd III welcomes renowned guests from all walks of public life (such as Diane Rehm, NPR host, at left) to engage in lively and* *thoughtful discussions on the major issues of the day in the light of Christian faith. The Sunday Forum is streamed live, archived, and viewable on-demand at www.nationalcathedral.org.*

✣ ABOVE: *EACH OCTOBER THE CATHEDRAL HOSTS THE Blessing of the Animals AS PART OF A CELEBRATION OF THE FEAST DAY OF St. FRANCIS OF ASSISI, WHO PRAYED, "ALL PRAISE TO YOU, OH LORD, FOR ALL THESE BROTHER AND SISTER CREATURES."*

✤ BELOW: *FLOWER MART,
AN ANNUAL EVENT HOSTED
BY ALL HALLOWS GUILD,
BRINGS VISITORS TO THE
CATHEDRAL CLOSE FROM ALL
AROUND THE REGION TO
SAMPLE VENDORS' WARES,
LEARN ABOUT GARDENING
AND THE ENVIRONMENT,* *AND TO ENJOY THE LUSH
GROUNDS OF THE CATHEDRAL.
FAMILY-FRIENDLY GAMES
AND RIDES, LIKE THE
CAROUSEL SHOWN HERE,
ROUND OUT THE FESTIVAL
EXPERIENCE.*

⟡ RIGHT: *BISHOPS FROM EPISCOPAL DIOCESES ALL OVER THE COUNTRY GATHERED AROUND JOHN BRYSON CHANE IN JUNE 2002, LAYING THEIR HANDS ON HIM AND JOINING IN THE PRAYER CONSECRATING HIM AS THE EIGHTH BISHOP OF WASHINGTON.*

⟡ RIGHT: *ARCHBISHOP DESMOND TUTU SPENT FIVE DAYS AT THE CATHEDRAL IN NOVEMBER 2007 AS PART OF THE CATHEDRAL'S CENTENNIAL CELEBRATION. IN ADDITION TO PREACHING, LECTURING, AND SERVING AS A GUEST FOR THE SUNDAY FORUM, ARCHBISHOP TUTU RECEIVED THE INAUGURAL CATHEDRAL PRIZE FOR ADVANCEMENT IN RELIGIOUS UNDERSTANDING IN RECOGNITION OF HIS LIFETIME OF WORK IN UNITING PEOPLE ACROSS THE GLOBE.*

⟡ LEFT: *THE CATHEDRAL SERVES THE NATION IN TIMES OF GREAT CELEBRATION AND MOURNING, PROVIDING A GATHERING PLACE FOR EVENTS OF NATIONAL SIGNIFICANCE, SUCH AS THE FUNERAL SERVICE FOR FORMER PRESIDENT GERALD R. FORD IN JANUARY 2007.*

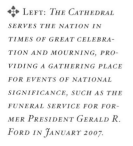

✤ RIGHT: *THE CATHEDRAL'S*
PENTECOST SERVICE IN 2008
CELEBRATES THE CULMINA-
TION OF ITS CENTENNIAL
YEAR AND THE BEGINNING OF
A NEW CENTURY OF MINISTRY.

✤ BELOW: *MEMBERS OF NEW*
YORK'S ST. PAUL COMMUNITY
BAPTIST CHURCH'S MAAFA
COMPANY EVOKE THE HORRORS
OF SLAVERY AND THE JOY OF
TRIUMPH OVER ADVERSITY IN
THE CATHEDRAL'S HURRICANE
KATRINA AID SERVICE.

✤ LEFT: *MUSIC IS AT THE*
CENTER OF THE CATHEDRAL'S
WORSHIP LIFE. OUR CHOIRS
ADORN OUR CELEBRATIONS
WITH SONG THROUGHOUT THE
YEAR AND SERVE AS ONE OF
THE HIGHLIGHTS OF A VISIT
TO THE CATHEDRAL.

✤ RIGHT: *A WEALTH OF*
MUSICAL TRADITIONS GRACE
CATHEDRAL SERVICES, LIFTING
VOICES IN SONG TO THE PRAISE
AND GLORY OF GOD'S NAME.

✤ ABOVE: *THE REV. DR. SAMUEL T. LLOYD III IS THE NINTH DEAN OF WASHINGTON NATIONAL CATHEDRAL, WHERE HE LEADS A NEW VISION FOR THE CATHEDRAL'S FUTURE SERVICE TO WASHINGTON, D.C., THE NATION, AND THE WORLD.*

AN EMERGING VOICE FOR A GENEROUS-SPIRITED CHRISTIANITY, HE PREACHES TWICE A MONTH AT THE CATHEDRAL, AND HIS SERMONS ARE AVAILABLE ONLINE AT WWW.NATIONAL CATHEDRAL.ORG.

✤ RIGHT: *THE CATHEDRAL'S CENTER FOR PRAYER AND PILGRIMAGE PRESENTS A MONTHLY OPPORTUNITY FOR SEEKERS TO WALK THE CATHEDRAL'S LABYRINTH IN THE TWILIGHT QUIET OF THE NAVE.*

General Information

November 1, 1890	Bishop William Paret responds favorably to inquiries about the possibility of an Episcopal Cathedral Foundation in Washington.
December 8, 1891	A meeting is held at the home of Charles C. Glover to discuss the possibility of an Episcopal cathedral and associated educational institutions in Washington.
January 6, 1893	President Benjamin Harrison signs the charter granted by an Act of Congress to establish the Protestant Episcopal Cathedral Foundation.
Annunciation Day, March 25, 1896	Henry Yates Satterlee is consecrated as the first Episcopal Bishop of Washington.
September 7, 1898	First tract of Mount St. Alban land is bought from Amzi I. and Julia L. Barber for $245,000.
October 23, 1898	First service is held on the grounds of the future Cathedral, as a Peace Cross is raised to give thanks for the founding of the Cathedral Church of St. Peter and St. Paul. President William McKinley addresses the crowd.
Ascension Day, May 1901	First in a series of open-air worship services is held on Mount St. Alban.
Thanksgiving 1905	Purchase of the site is completed, as the mortgage is paid in full.
June 10, 1907	The architectural plans of George Bodley and Henry Vaughan are approved by the Cathedral Chapter.
Michaelmas, September 29, 1907	Foundation Stone laid; dedication of the Canterbury Pulpit.
October 21, 1907	Architect George Bodley dies.
March 31, 1910	First meeting of the National Cathedral Association
All Saints Day, November 1, 1910	Laying of the corner stone and dedication of Bethlehem Chapel.
May 1, 1912	Bethlehem Chapel opens and the first service is held within the Cathedral.
1916	All Hallows Guild is founded.
June 30, 1917	Architect Henry Vaughan dies.
November 1921	Cathedral Chapter designates the firm of Froham, Robb & Little as Cathedral architects.
Summer, 1926	Bishop's Garden is opened.
1927	Completion of the crypt chapels of St. Joseph of Arimathea and Resurrection.
Fall 1929	College of Preachers is dedicated.
May 16, 1930	Pilgrim Steps are dedicated.

✤ Top: *Bishop Henry Yates Satterlee with the Board of Trustees, 1901.* Above: *Florence Bratenahl with members of All Hallows Guild, 1923*

✣ Above: *Early proces-*
sion up the Pilgrim
Steps. Below Top:
Altar Guild head Lucy
Mackrille. Below
Bottom: *The dedication*
of the Space window

May 1932	Formal opening of the choir, sanctuary, and North Transept
October 1940	The Cathedral is designated as the seat of the Presiding Bishop of the Episcopal Church of the United States of America. From this date, presiding bishops are installed in a ceremony at the Cathedral.
December 1941	Cathedral holds an interfaith service following America's entry into World War II.
May 13, 1942	Debut of the Cathedral Choral Society
May 14, 1942	Dedication of the Women's Porch of the North Transept
February 15, 1952	Memorial service for Great Britain's King George VI
1954	Formation of the Cathedral's National Needlepoint Committee
1956	Dedication of the High Altar and the Wilson Bay
October 20, 1957	Dedication of the War Memorial Chapel in the presence of President Dwight Eisenhower and Queen Elizabeth II
1957	Richard T. Feller is appointed Clerk of the Works. He will oversee the building of the Cathedral through the completion of the structure in 1990.
November 18, 1962	Dedication of the south transept
September 22, 1963	Dedication of the Kibbey Memorial Carillon
Ascension Day, May 7, 1964	Dedication of the Gloria in Excelsis Tower
March 31, 1968	The Rev. Dr. Martin Luther King, Jr., preaches his last Sunday sermon before being assassinated four days later.
March 28, 1969	Funeral service for President Dwight D. Eisenhower
October 31, 1971	Dedication of the South Portal
November 2, 1971	President Indira Ghandi of India speaks at the Cathedral during a state visit.
October 30, 1972	Death of Cathedral architect Philip Hubert Frohman
January 5, 1973	Memorial service for President Harry S. Truman
January 19, 1973	Leonard Bernstein conducts the National Symphony Orchestra in Hadyn's *Mass in Time of War*, as thousands attend in the Nave and outside on the Close.
November 9, 1973	*Majestus* is installed in the High Altar reredos.
July 21, 1974	Dedication of the *Space* window, with the participation of Apollo 11 astronauts Buzz Aldrin, Neil Armstrong, and Michael Collins
1976	Dedication of the nave and unveiling of the west rose window
September 29, 1982	Service held celebrating the Cathedral's seventy-fifth anniversary of its founding; dedication of the Pilgrim Observation Gallery.
October 2, 1982	Dedication of the *Ex Nihilo* tympanum
December 17, 1987	Last of the 112 gargoyles adorning the Cathedral installed on the St. Peter Tower.
September 30, 1989	Year of Consecration and Dedication begins. Bishop John T. Walker dies.
May 5, 1990	The Diocese of Washington pinnacle is completed with the setting of its finial stone. Parishioners and choristers from throughout the Diocese participate, as the West Portal Court is dedicated in memory of Bishop John Walker.
September 29, 1990	The Cathedral is physically completed with the setting of its last stone, the finial of the National Cathedral Association pinnacle on the south (St. Paul) Tower, while thousands watch. It is eighty-three years to the day from the setting of the Foundation Stone.

SEPTEMBER 30, 1990	The Cathedral Church of St. Peter and St. Paul, Washington National Cathedral, is officially consecrated as "a great church for national purposes" and "a house of prayer for all people."
JANUARY 14, 1991	Eight thousand attend an interfaith peace service and candlelight vigil prior to the start of the First Gulf War.
OCTOBER 1992	An historic Columbus Day celebration includes representatives of indigenous peoples from the U.S., Canada, Central and South America, the Philippines, New Zealand, and Japan.
NOVEMBER 1992	Cathedral forum on challenges confronting the global climate and the environment
JANUARY 28, 1993	Funeral of Supreme Court Justice Thurgood Marshall
APRIL 29, 1993	First visit of Tenzin Gyatso, the fourteenth Dalai Lama, who will visit the Cathedral on numerous subsequent occasions.
OCTOBER 9, 1994	Archbishop Desmond Tutu preaches at a Cathedral service celebrating the newly democratic government of South Africa.
FEBRUARY 1995	The Cathedral is the first religious institution invited to participate in the Philadelphia Flower Show. A special prize is created to honor the Cathedral Altar Guild's presentation.
OCTOBER 1995	The first national symposium on pastoral care and AIDS is held at the Cathedral.
SEPTEMBER 6, 1997	Memorial service is held for Diana, Princess of Wales.
SEPTEMBER 11, 1998	Memorial service is held for the victims of the bombing of the U.S. embassies in Kenya and Tanzania.
JANUARY 2000	President and Mrs. Bill Clinton participate in a Holy Eucharist service to greet the Millennium.
SEPTEMBER 14, 2001	The Cathedral hosts an interfaith National Day of Prayer and Remembrance to honor those killed in the terrorist attacks on September 11.
MAY 29, 2004	Service to celebrate the dedication of the National World War II Memorial
JUNE 11, 2004	Funeral service for President Ronald W. Reagan
SEPTEMBER 1, 2004	The College of Preachers and the Cathedral's Program Department merge to form the Cathedral College.
FEBRUARY 3, 2006	An interfaith service is held to launch fundraising efforts for the rebuilding of New Orleans following Hurricane Katrina.
SEPTEMBER 7, 2006	Former Iranian president Mohammed Khatami speaks on seeking greater dialogue between the nations of the world.
NOVEMBER 5, 2006	Seating of The Most Reverend Dr. Katharine Jefferts Schori, first female primate of the Episcopal Church of the United States of America
JANUARY 2, 2007	Funeral service for President Gerald R. Ford
SEPTEMBER 29, 2007	The beginning of a year-long celebration of the Centennial of Washington National Cathedral.
OCTOBER 2007	Introduction of the Sunday Forum, a weekly discussion among leaders from various disciplines of the critical issues of the day in the light of faith
NOVEMBER 2007	The Most Rev. Dr. Desmond M. Tutu, Archbishop Emeritus of South Africa, is awarded the inaugural Cathedral Prize for Advancement in Religious Understanding.

✣ ABOVE: *THE INSTAL-LATION OF THE LAST GARGOYLE.* BELOW TOP: *THE DALAI LAMA SPEAKING AT THE CATHEDRAL.* BELOW BOTTOM: *THE FUNERAL OF PRESIDENT GERALD R. FORD*

GLOSSARY OF TERMS

Ambulatory   A passage behind the altar separated from the latter by columns or piers

Apse   The semicircular, or polygonal, termination of the sanctuary of a church

Arcade   A range of arches, supported on piers or columns, either open or closed with masonry

Archivolt   The decorated molding around the face of an arch, often decorated

Balustrade   A low wall or railing of stone to protect the edge of a platform, balcony, or roof

Barrel vault   A simple form of tunnel-like vaulting deriving its name from its resemblance to a half-barrel

Bay   A division or compartment in the arrangement of a building that consists of a pair of piers linked by a pointed arch, with triforium openings, a clerestory window, and a section of the vaulted ceiling above

Boss   A projecting stone at the intersection of ribs, frequently elaborately carved, the function of which is to provide a net intersection of the ribs and join them into one unit

Buttress   A masonry member projecting from a wall, rising from the ground, and counteracting the outward thrust of the roof or vaulting; characteristic of Gothic architecture, a flying buttress is a freestanding element connected by an arch to the outer wall.

Canon   A member of the cathedral staff, under the rule of the bishop

Canopy   A protective awning or roof above statues

Capital   The upper part of a column, pier, or pilaster, which is frequently decorated by carved animals and foliage

Cathedra   The seat of a bishop

Cenotaph   A monument to the memory of a person whose body is buried elsewhere

Chancel   The part of the church that contains the choir and the sanctuary

Chapter   The governing board of a cathedral

Cinquefoil   A figure of five equal segments composed of converging arcs

Clerestory   That portion of the wall rising above the triforium level, or roofs, of the aisles. It is pierced by windows usually of large size.

Cloister   Covered passages linking the church with separate buildings, or arcaded passages around an open space

Close   The area on which a cathedral and subordinate buildings stand

Columbarium   A structure of vaults lined with recesses for urns and caskets

Column   An upright circular shaft; usually tapered, standing on a base and surmounted by a capital

Corbel   A projection from the face of a wall, supporting a beam, vaulting shaft, or a piece of statuary

Credence   The shelf or table at the side of the sanctuary upon which are placed the bread and wine for the Holy Communion

Crocket   An ornament consisting of a projecting piece of sculptured stone or wood that decorates the sloping ridges of gablets, spires, and pinnacles; usually carved as foliage with a strong stem or rib

Crossing   The space created by the intersection of nave, transepts, and choir

Crypt   A vaulted space or passageway beneath a church

Dean   The officer in charge of the worship and administration of a cathedral

Dentils   One of a series of small projecting rectangular blocks forming a molding, especially under a cornice

Drip mould   An outside projecting piece of stone, often decoratively carved, shaped, or placed to throw off rain and prevent the rain from running down walls

Façade   The whole exterior of a cathedral or building (or, more strictly, the principal front of the structure), as seen in one view

Finial	The topmost portion of a pinnacle, usually sculptured as an elaborate ornament with upright stem and cluster of crockets. Seen at a distance, it resembles a cross from any angle of vision.
Frieze	A band of richly ornamented sculpture that decorates architecture or furniture
Frontal	A cloth, usually of silk or damask, that hangs in front of the altar and reaches the floor
Gablet	A small ornamental gable
Gargoyle	Carved into the image of a beast or ugly creature, a pierced or tunneled stone projecting from a gutter and intended to carry rain away from walls and foundations
Garth cloister	An enclosure surrounded by covered walkways, usually attached to a cathedral as a place of retreat
Gothic architecture	The style of architecture that originated in twelfth-century France and lasted into the sixteenth century during the high and late medieval period. Its characteristic features include the pointed arch, the ribbed vault, and the flying buttress.
Grotesque	A stone projecting from a building that serves to wick water away from the walls of the structure. Usually carved stone, a grotesque can take the form of a person, an ugly creature, or a soaring angel.
Label mould termination	Decoratively carved, large stone at the lower end of a moulding that defines an arch, window, or doorway
Lancet	A pointed arched window of one opening frequently arranged in groups of two to five
Lectern	The stand upon which the Bible is placed
Mullion	A vertical support or divider of panels, doors, or windows when set in a series
Multifoil	A flat object or opening with scalloped edges or ornaments
Nave	The body of the church building in which the congregation sits
Neo-Gothic	An architectural movement that began in the 1840s in England, when admirers of the Gothic style sought to revive medieval forms
Niche	A recess in the face of a wall or pier, prepared to receive a statue
Parapet	A low wall or railing to protect the edge of a platform, roof, or bridge
Pier	A mass of masonry supporting an arch or vault and distinct from a column. A clustered pier is composed of a number of small columns.
Pilaster	A slightly-projecting column, ornamental in function, built into or onto a wall to give the appearance of a weight-bearing support.
Pinnacle	A turret tapering upward to the top, its gracefulness enhanced by crockets and a top stone called a finial
Pointed arch	An arch formed by the intersection of two segments of a circle
Porch	A small vestibule where one can pause before entering another room
Portal	A major entrance to a church, emphasized by sculpture and decoration
Predella	The step or platform on which an altar is placed, or the lowest part of a reredos, immediately above the altar; also, the lowest part of a stained glass window
Provost	The chief clergyman of a cathedral when the bishop serves as dean
Quatrefoil	A figure used in window tracery, shaped to form a cross or four equal segments of a circle
Reredos	The wall or a screen at the back of an altar, either in carved stone, wood, or metal work
Rib	A projecting band, originally running along the groin of a vault. In Gothic architecture, ribs emphasize upward movement and serve both an aesthetic and structural function. The ridge rib follows the ridge of the roof, which is the uppermost horizontal line.
Rood beam	A large beam set transversely across a church from north to south on which stands a crucifix
Rood screen	The ornamental screen that separates the nave from the choir and sanctuary and serves metaphorically to separate the world from heaven

Rose window	A round window, with tracery dividing it into sections, often called petals. The Gothic rose is a development of the Romanesque wheel window, which symbolized Christ as the sun.
Sanctuary	The eastern part of a church immediately surrounding the High Altar
Sedilia	Seats in the sanctuary near the altar, usually three in number, for the clergy
Spandrel	The space between any arch or curved brace and the level or beam over the same
Tomb	A grave or monument erected to enclose the body and preserve the name and memory of the dead
Tracery	A term for the variations of mullions in Gothic windows and for geometric systems on wall panels and doors
Transept	Either of the two arms, north and south, of a church built in the form of a cross
Triforium	The middle level of a three-division vertical bay in a Gothic cathedral; an arcade gallery between the sloping roof over the aisles and aisle vaulting
Triptych	A picture, design, or carving of three panels; often an altar piece
Trompette en Chamade	Powerfully voiced reed stops in a pipe organ, mounted horizontally rather than vertically, that project into the church; used for fanfares and solos because of their commanding trumpet-like tone
Trumeau	A column in the center of two adjoining doors that support the tympanum above
Turret	A small tower usually corbelled from a corner
Tympanum	Usually decorated in rich sculpture, the space contained within a pointed or round arch above a Gothic portal
Vesica	An aureole, or pointed oval shape, surrounding a sacred image
Voussior	One of the wedge-shaped stones forming the curved parts of an arch or vaulted ceiling

BISHOPS OF THE EPISCOPAL DIOCESE OF WASHINGTON

Henry Yates Satterlee, 1896–1908

Alfred Harding, 1909–1923

James E. Freeman, 1923–1943

Angus Dun, 1944–1962

William F. Creighton, 1962–1977

John T. Walker, 1977–1989

Ronald H. Haines, 1990–2000

John B. Chane, 2002–present

DEANS OF WASHINGTON NATIONAL CATHEDRAL

Alfred Harding, 1908–1915

George C. F. Bratenahl, 1916–1936

Noble C. Powell, 1937–1941

Zebarney T. Phillips, 1941–1942

John W. Suter, 1944–1950

Francis B. Sayre, Jr., 1951–1978

John T. Walker, 1978–1989

Nathan D. Baxter, 1992–2003

Samuel T. Lloyd III, 2005–present

William F. Amole

Isabel Anderson

Larz Anderson

Eleanor Bell Arterton

Frederick Harry Arterton

Lillian Cox Athey

Thomas Franklin Athey

Beatrice E. Wilson Baker

Iraline Green Barnes

William Ashby Beal

William Tapley Bennett, Jr.

James Platte Berkeley

Mabel Thorp Boardman

Franklin Johns Bohanan

Jennie P. Bohanan

Florence Brown Bratenahl

George Carl Fitch Bratenahl

Olivia Southwell Brown

Charles Francis Burton

Paul Smith Callaway

Julia Grant Cantacuzene

Leonard Carmichael

Pearl Kidston Carmichael

Louis Welborn Cassels

Charles Thomas Clagett, Jr.

Nancy Leiter Clagett

Mary Gantt Claggett

Thomas John Claggett

William Brown Crawford

Marie-Louise Creighton

William Forman Creighton

Joseph Edward Davies

William Levering De Vries

Frederick Ward Denys

Mabel Eaton Denys

George Dewey

Mildred McLean Dewey

Joan Shaw Dirksen

Richard Wayne Dirksen

Carolyn DuBois Cosby Dorsey

Stephen P. Dorsey

Mary Mann DuBose

William J. DuBose, Sr.

Angus Dun

Catherine W. Dun

Thomas Oman Edmunds

Leonard Webster Ellinwood

Lera Slayback Ellinwood

Edward Fall

Helen M. Fall

Italo Fanfani

Richard Tabler Feller

Wilma Stenger Feller

Sally Van Horn Finney

Thomas Dunn Finney, Jr.

John Clifford Folger

Kathrine Dulin Folger

Charles Sidney Forbes

Ramona Frances Blunt Forbes

Ella Vigelius Freeman

James Edward Freeman

Olivia Frohman

Philip Hubert Frohman

F. Elizabeth Fry

Phillip Hayes Funkhouser

Sanford Garner, Jr.

Ethel Shields Garrett

George Angus Garrett

Charles Leslie Glenn

Patricia S. Gow

Thomas M. Gow

Elizabeth Smith Green

Ethel T. Green

Walter Irving Green

Ernest W. Greene

Ronald H. Haines

Alfred Harding

Douglas Harding

Justine Prindle Harding

Elizabeth M. Hartson

Nelson Thomas Hartson

Vera C. Hartson

Caroline Klotz Herod

William Rogers Herod

George Burton Hotchkiss, Jr.

Katherine Piercy Howard

Margaret Hughes Howard

Cordell Hull

Rose Witz Hull

Frank Ronaldson Jelleff

Margaret Gollan Jelleff

Coleman Jennings

Carmen Mabel Atwell Johnson

Lent Clifton Johnson

Margaret Elizabeth Bayer Jones

Ralph Anson Jones

Helen Keller

Clara M. Kellogg

Frank Billings Kellogg

Benjamin King, Jr.

Marjorie Brown King

John Sumner Koch

Herman Henry Kohlsaat

Irene Matz LeCompte

Norma B. Lewis

Robert Lee Lewis

Willmett Lewis

Breckinridge Long

Christine Graham Long

Grace E. Long

James Minor Ludlow

Lucy Vaughan Mackrille

Anne Sullivan Macy

Cornelia Marshall

John Fellows Marshall

Charles Samuel Martin

Edith Sturges Martin

Lea Martin Massi

Leonore Knight Williams McKnew

Thomas Willson McKnew

Virginia Paff McKnew

Georgene Armstrong Davis McTigue

John William McTigue

Antonio A. Micocci

George Gardner Monks

Katherine Knowles Monks

A. S. Mike Monroney

Mary Ellen Monroney

Louise Kavakos Morigi

Roger Morigi

Robert Cunningham Morton

Ruth Whelden Morton

John R. Mott

Gertrude Walden Myer

Walden Myer

Alma White O'Brian

John Lord O'Brian

Katherine Baillie Olin

Philip James Olin

Alice Maury Parmelee

James Parmelee

Sallie Hews Phillips

ZeBarney Thorne Phillips

Henry Homes Porter ➤

Mary Kinney Porter
Edgar Priest
Edith Morgan Priest
Abigail Norman Prince
Frederick Henry Prince
Norman Prince
Molly Pagan Purdy
Mary Frederica Rives
Clyde Christian Roth
Gertrude de la Barthe Steele Roth
Ferdinand Edward Ruge
Louise Baldwin Ruge
Anna Embury Sheldon Russell
James Townsend Russell
Harry Lee Rust, Jr.
Mildred Anderson Rust
Henry Yates Satterlee
Jane Lawrence Satterlee
Elizabeth E. Sayre
Francis Bowes Sayre, Sr.
Harriet Hart Sayre
Douglas McKain Scott
Constantine Leonidas Seferlis
Marion Andrus Seferlis
Adelaide Sheldon

Albert James Sheldon
Allen Jairus Sheldon
Eliza Denton Sheldon
Harriette Chandler Sheldon
Agnes Hann Smith
James Gibson Smith
Mary Elizabeth Smith
John Wesley Snyder
Leo Sowerby
Melville Elijah Stone
Alice Trowbridge Strong
Lester Corrin Strong
Carolyn Hall Sturgis
Philip Beach Sullivan
Evelyn Wadsworth Symington
William Stuart Symington
Mary Agnes (Polly) Thomson
Robert S. Trenbath
Alexander Buel Trowbridge
Alexander Buel Trowbridge, Jr.
Gertrude Sherman Trowbridge
Katherine Lester Trowbridge
Louise Thorne Trowbridge
Sherman Trowbridge
Stephen Van Renssalaer Trowbridge

Henry Vaughan
John Thomas Walker
R. Gordon Wasson
Thomas C. Wasson
Cynthia Clark Wedel
Theodore O. Wedel
Irwin Harold Wensink
Margaret Crossant Wensink
Elizabeth Moffat White
Henry White
John Campbell White
Margaret Stuyvesant Rutherford White
Lucy Ogden Williams
Merritt Francis Williams
Margaret G. Wilmer
Re Lewis Wilmer
Richard Hooker Wilmer
Richard Hooker Wilmer, Jr.
William Holland Wilmer
Edith Bolling Wilson
Woodrow Wilson
Harriet Wright
J. Butler Wright
Lillian M. A. Yeo

FOR FURTHER READING

Jewels of Light: The Stained Glass of Washington National Cathedral by Elody R. Crimi and Diane Ney with photographs by Ken Cobb; Washington National Cathedral, Washington, DC, 2004, 206 pages.

Guide to Gargoyles and Other Grotesques by Wendy True Gasch with photographs by Robert Llewellyn; Washington National Cathedral, Washington, DC, 2003, 122 pages.

The Stone Carvers: Master Craftsmen of Washington National Cathedral by Marjorie Hunt; Smithsonian Institution Press, Washington, DC, and London, 1999, 208 pages.

The Art of Gothic: Architecture, Sculpture, Painting, edited by Rolf Tomen with photographs by Achim Bednorz; Könemann Publishing, New York, 2004, 520 pages.

How to Read a Church: A Guide to Images, Symbols and Meaning in Churches and Cathedrals by Richard Taylor; Paulist Press, Mahwah, New Jersey, 2005, 224 pages.

Stained Glass: From Its Origins to the Present by Virginia Chieffo Raguin; Harry N. Abrams, Inc., New York, 2003, 288 pages.

Great Cathedrals by Bernhard Shütz with photographs by Albert Hirmer, Florian Monheim, and Joseph Martin; Harry N. Abrams, Inc., New York, 2002, 460 pages.

A Treasury of Anglican Art by James B. Simpson and George H. Eatman; Rizzoli International Publications, New York, 2002, 224 pages.

Gothic Architecture by Paul Frankl, revised by Paul Crossley; Yale University Press, New Haven, Connecticut, 2001, 480 pages.

A Sculptor's Fortunes by Walker Hancock with Edward Connery Lathem; Cape Ann Historical Association, Gloucester, Massachusetts, 1997, 277 pages.

The House of God: Church Architecture, Style and History by Edward Norman; Thames and Hudson, 1990, 144 pages.

Art and Beauty in the Middle Ages by Umberto Eco; Yale University Press, New Haven, 1986, 131 pages.

The Age of the Cathedrals: Art and Society, 980–1420 by Georges Duby, The University of Chicago Press, 1981, 311 pages.

Illustrated Dictionary of Historic Architecture edited by Cyril M. Harris; Dover Publications, Inc., New York, 1977, 592 pages.

High Gothic by Hans Jantzen, Princeton University Press, Princeton, New Jersey, 1984, 181 pages.

Books in this list may be purchased by calling 1-800-319-7073 or the Cathedral Museum Store website at www.nationalcathedral.org.

GREAT CATHEDRALS
Dimensions in feet

	Length	Span of nave	Height of nave	Area in square feet
St. Peter's, Rome	718'	—	150'	227,069'
Seville	430'	—	150'	128,570'
St. John, New York	601'	48'	124'	121,000'
Liverpool	619'	50'	116'	101,000'
Milan	475'	56'	153'	92,600'
Washington	518'	41'	104'	83,012'
Amiens	435'	46'	144'	71,208'
Chartres	507'	52'	122'	68,260'
Cologne	427'	41'	155'	65,800'
Rheims	430'	48'	125'	65,000'
Notre Dame	426'	45'	110'	64,108'

WASHINGTON NATIONAL CATHEDRAL

NOTRE DAME

MILAN

ST. PETER'S

LIVERPOOL

AMIENS

CHARTRES

ST. JOHN

RHEIMS

SEVILLE

COLOGNE

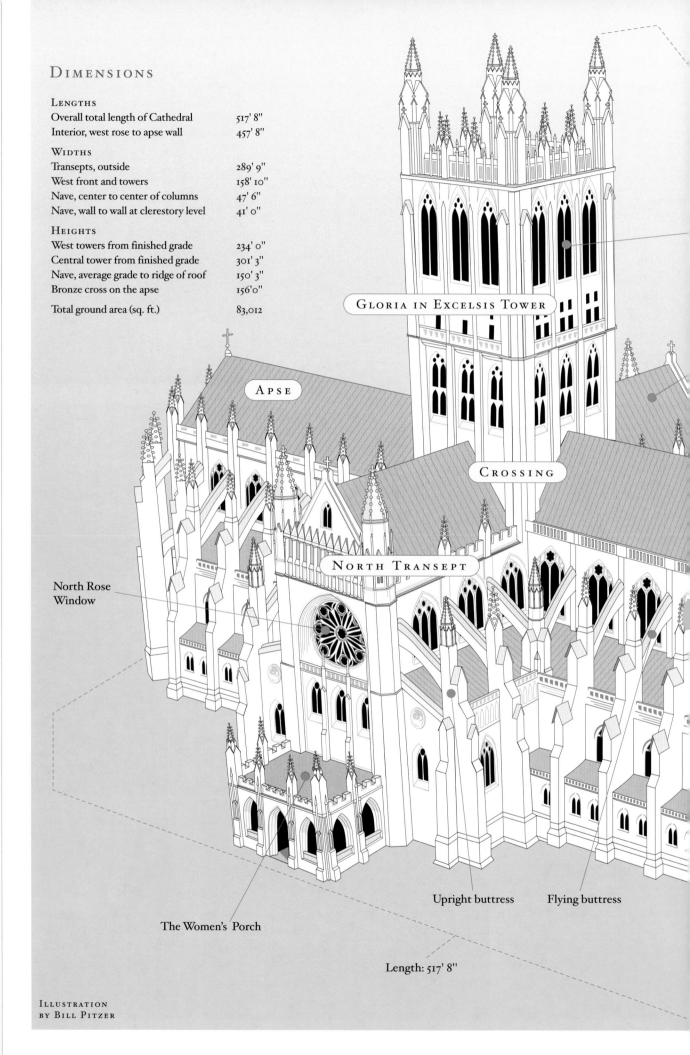

Dimensions

Lengths

Overall total length of Cathedral	517' 8"
Interior, west rose to apse wall	457' 8"

Widths

Transepts, outside	289' 9"
West front and towers	158' 10"
Nave, center to center of columns	47' 6"
Nave, wall to wall at clerestory level	41' 0"

Heights

West towers from finished grade	234' 0"
Central tower from finished grade	301' 3"
Nave, average grade to ridge of roof	150' 3"
Bronze cross on the apse	156'0"
Total ground area (sq. ft.)	83,012

GLORIA IN EXCELSIS TOWER

APSE

CROSSING

NORTH TRANSEPT

North Rose
Window

Upright buttress   Flying buttress

The Women's Porch

Length: 517' 8"

ILLUSTRATION
BY BILL PITZER

The Cathedral Exterior

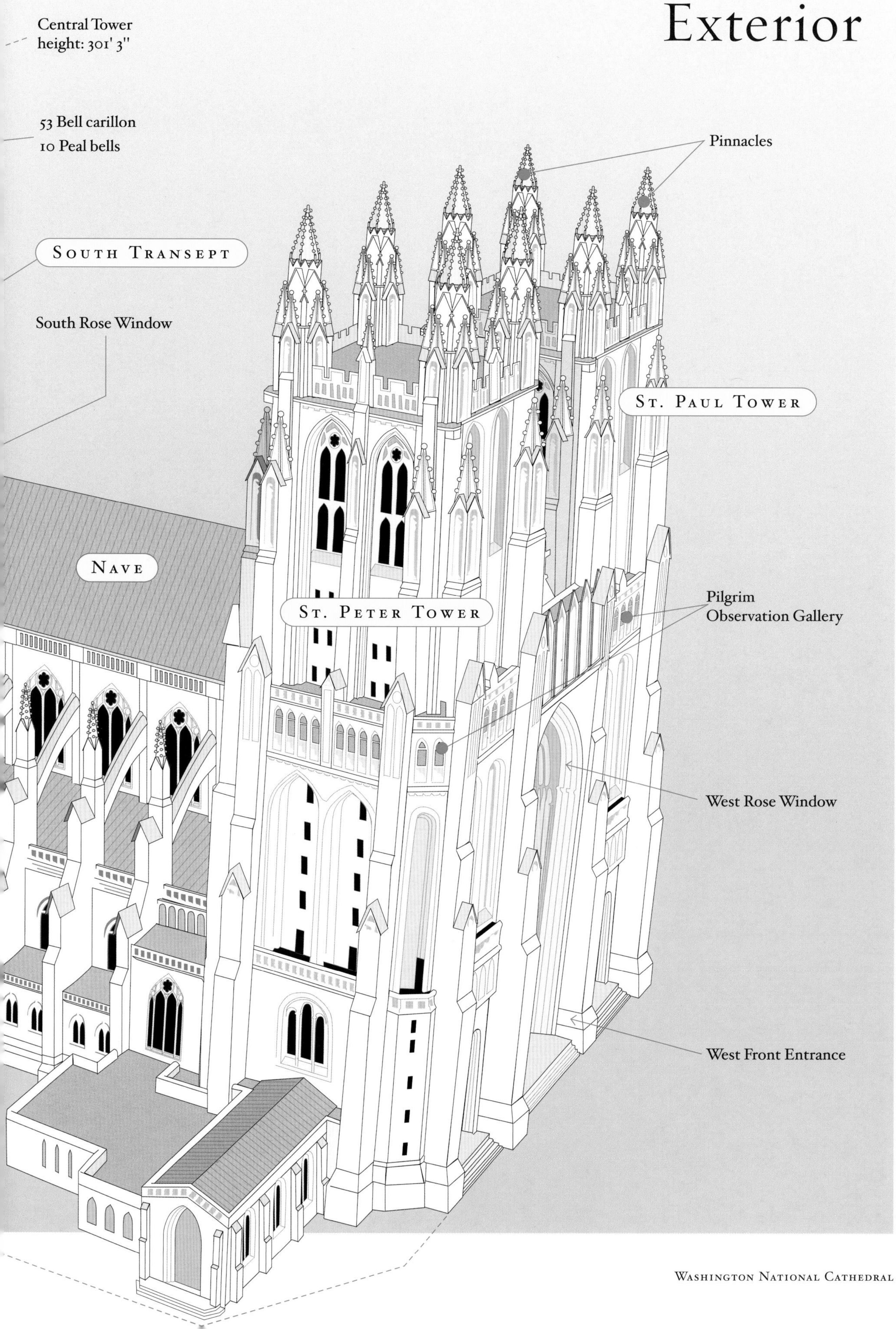

Central Tower
height: 301' 3"

53 Bell carillon
10 Peal bells

Pinnacles

SOUTH TRANSEPT

South Rose Window

ST. PAUL TOWER

NAVE

ST. PETER TOWER

Pilgrim
Observation Gallery

West Rose Window

West Front Entrance

Cross Section

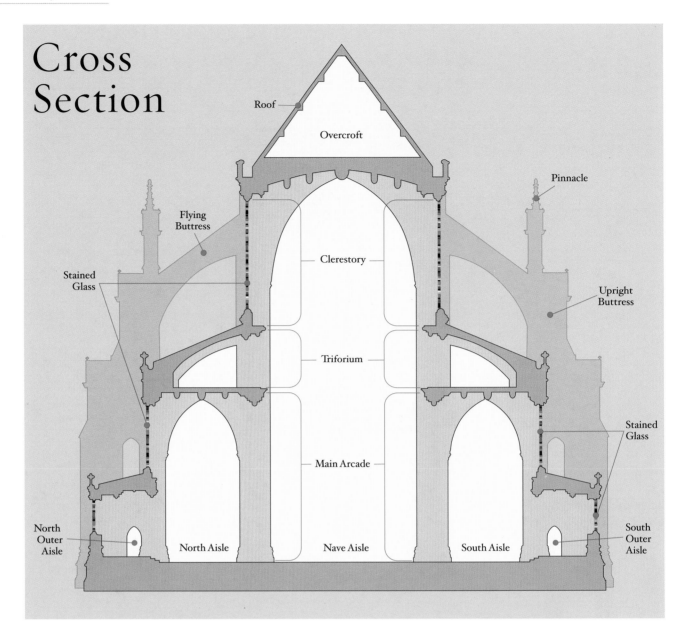

Roof

Overcroft

Pinnacle

Flying Buttress

Clerestory

Stained Glass

Upright Buttress

Triforium

Main Arcade

Stained Glass

North Outer Aisle

North Aisle

Nave Aisle

South Aisle

South Outer Aisle

CONSTRUCTION TIMELINE

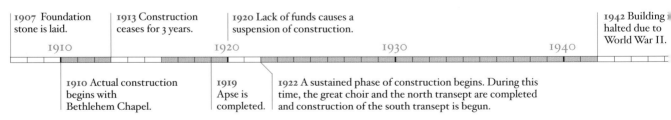

1907 Foundation stone is laid.

1913 Construction ceases for 3 years.

1920 Lack of funds causes a suspension of construction.

1942 Building halted due to World War II.

1910

1920

1930

1940

1910 Actual construction begins with Bethlehem Chapel.

1919 Apse is completed.

1922 A sustained phase of construction begins. During this time, the great choir and the north transept are completed and construction of the south transept is begun.

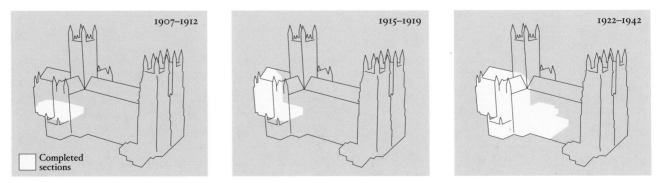

1907–1912

1915–1919

1922–1942

Completed sections

Nave Elevations

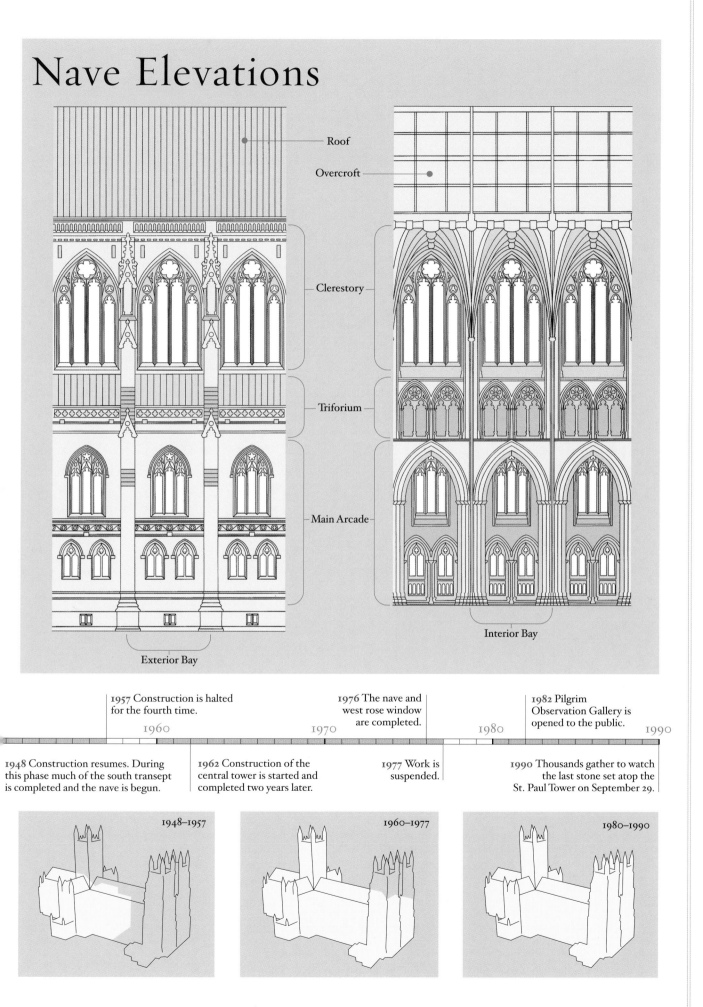

Roof

Overcroft

Clerestory

Triforium

Main Arcade

Interior Bay

Exterior Bay

1957 Construction is halted for the fourth time.

1976 The nave and west rose window are completed.

1982 Pilgrim Observation Gallery is opened to the public.

1960   1970   1980   1990

1948 Construction resumes. During this phase much of the south transept is completed and the nave is begun.

1962 Construction of the central tower is started and completed two years later.

1977 Work is suspended.

1990 Thousands gather to watch the last stone set atop the St. Paul Tower on September 29.

1948–1957

1960–1977

1980–1990

Main Level

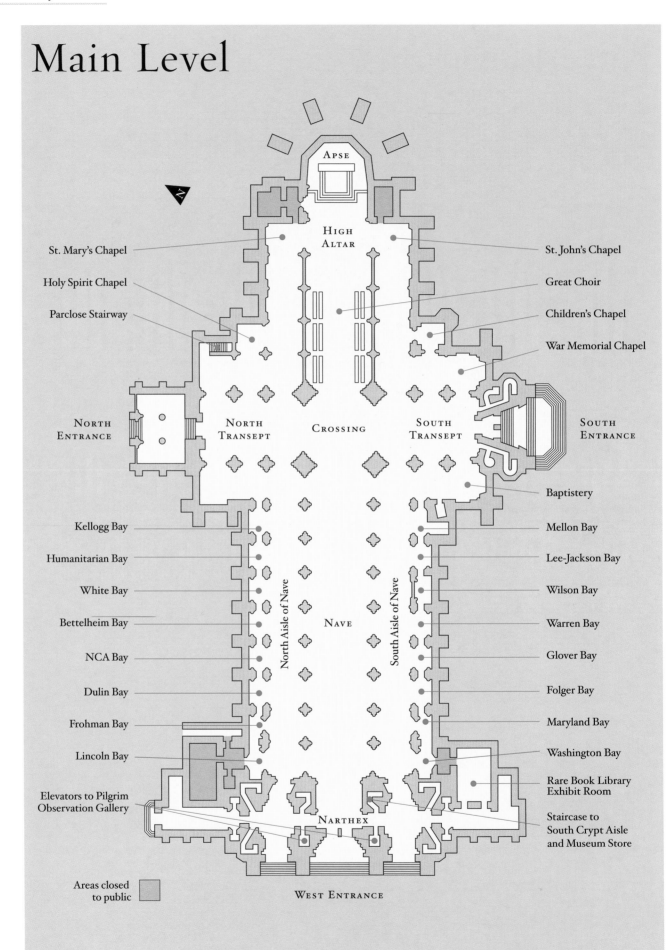

APSE

HIGH ALTAR

St. Mary's Chapel

St. John's Chapel

Holy Spirit Chapel

Great Choir

Parclose Stairway

Children's Chapel

War Memorial Chapel

NORTH ENTRANCE

NORTH TRANSEPT

CROSSING

SOUTH TRANSEPT

SOUTH ENTRANCE

Baptistery

Kellogg Bay

Mellon Bay

Humanitarian Bay

Lee-Jackson Bay

White Bay

Wilson Bay

Bettelheim Bay

Warren Bay

North Aisle of Nave

South Aisle of Nave

NCA Bay

NAVE

Glover Bay

Dulin Bay

Folger Bay

Frohman Bay

Maryland Bay

Lincoln Bay

Washington Bay

Elevators to Pilgrim Observation Gallery

Rare Book Library Exhibit Room

NARTHEX

Staircase to South Crypt Aisle and Museum Store

Areas closed to public

WEST ENTRANCE

Lower Level

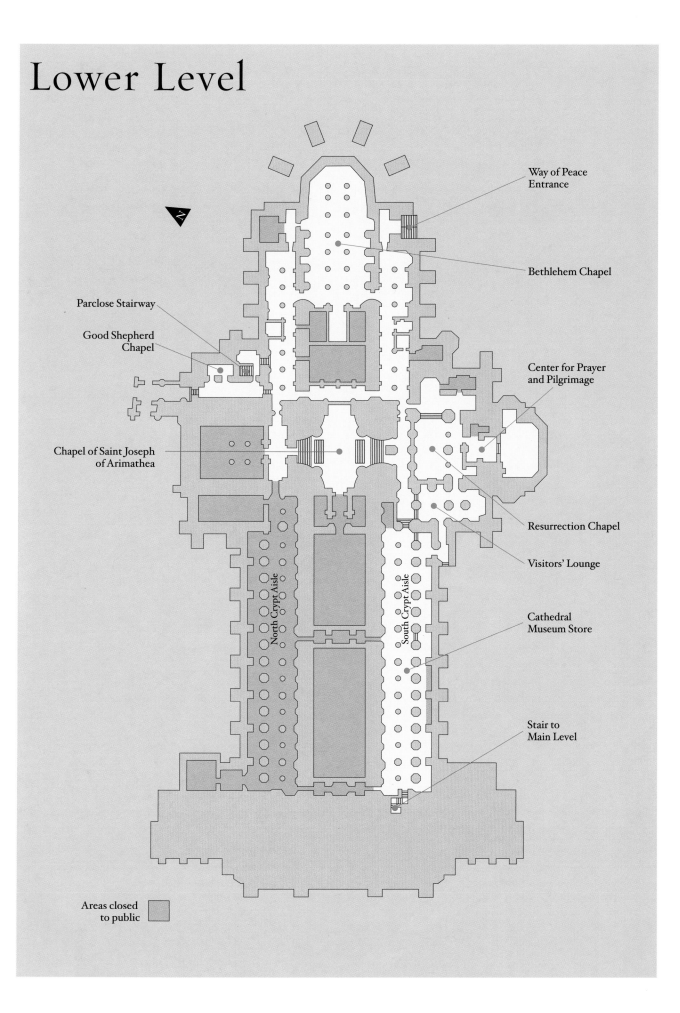

Way of Peace
Entrance

Bethlehem Chapel

Parclose Stairway

Good Shepherd
Chapel

Center for Prayer
and Pilgrimage

Chapel of Saint Joseph
of Arimathea

Resurrection Chapel

Visitors' Lounge

North Crypt Aisle

South Crypt Aisle

Cathedral
Museum Store

Stair to
Main Level

Areas closed
to public

The Close

1. Washington National Cathedral
2. Garth
3. Administration Building
4. Cathedral College
5. Cathedral Library
6. Sayre House
7. Pilgrim Steps
8. Bishop's Garden
9. Herb Cottage
10. Episcopal Church House
11. St. Alban's Church
12. Amphitheater
13. Olmsted Woods and Pilgrim Way
14. St. Albans School for Boys
15. School athletic fields
16. Beauvoir School
17. National Cathedral School for Girls
18. Underground parking garage and Security Office

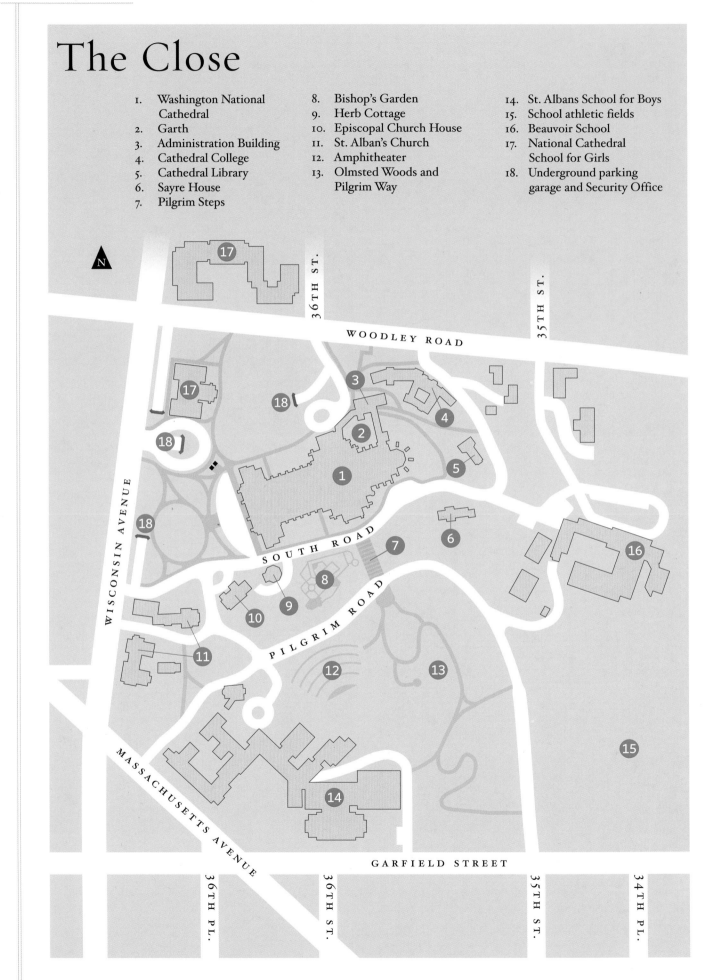